PROTECTION TECHNOLOGY:
VENDOR SELECTION & NIGHTMARE AVOIDANCE

PROTECTION TECHNOLOGY:
VENDOR SELECTION & NIGHTMARE AVOIDANCE

By: Timothy M. O'Brien, CPP

Criminal Intelligence Administration
3811 Ditmars Boulevard
Astoria, New York 11105
www.protect.nyc

Ordering Information:

Quantity sales. Special discounts are available on quantity purchases by corporations, associations, and others. For details, contact the publisher at the address above.

Orders by U.S. trade bookstores and wholesalers. Please contact Criminal Intelligence Administration: Tel: (800) 792.7181 or (718) 541-0723; Fax: (718) 504-7530 or visit www.protect.nyc.

Printed in the United States of America

TABLE OF CONTENTS

PREFACE

In today's world, threats from organized terrorists, lone-wolf actors and the "ordinary" criminal element readily pose a clear and present danger to ourselves, loved-ones, friends and associates. Daily, the newspapers are filled with stories from around the globe detailing horrific acts perpetrated against civilians to further religious, political or economic goals. Unfortunately, this is our reality.

We as a society in general must take steps to protect both ourselves and family from those wishing to cause us harm. Yes, sounds simple and it is an absolute given. Let's take it a step further. In addition to responsibilities for our family, we are in a responsible charge position at work. Whether a property manager, board member, property owner, security director or any similar title, we are also responsible for the protection of our respective property.

This publication provides a cradle-to-grave, systematic procedure you can initiate in order to protect the properties and facilities under your control. This time-proven methodology has been a proprietary process I have utilized since my consulting practice was established back in 1987. Our process begins with an overview of the current threats, moves through our legal obligations, continues with a vulnerability assessment for your particular property, streamlines the development of the request for proposals and ends with the final phase of project management.

This publication is intended to help the reader not only protect their properties but deal more effectively with contractors. Included are real-life pitfalls and project disasters I have witnessed first-hand.

The Threat Overview

As professionals charged with the protection of persons occupying or otherwise conducting business within commercial and residential properties we must remain ever so vigilant of the current and continuing threats facing us today. These threats, range from a variety of sources such as organized terrorist entities to the "low-level" street criminals. These threats leave our properties and residents vulnerable and susceptible to property loss, injury and even death.

Terrorism

As yet another anniversary of the attacks on the United States approaches, it provides a time for not only somber reflection - but reflection on what new and emerging threats have come to light. The 2009 bomb plot by Hosam Maher Husein Smadi, a 19 year old Jordanian national living illegally within the United States, to detonate an explosive device at the base of the Fountain Place office tower in Dallas Texas underscores the threats facing us today. The recent attacks in Boston, Massachusetts and the operations directed and inspired by the Islamic State of Iraq and the Levant (ISIL) in Paris, San Bernardino, Brussels, Orlando and Turkey have once again brought to the forefront the radicalization of individuals within the United States and allied countries. These individuals have proven to be effective terror machines utilizing nothing but assault rifles and home-made improvised explosive devices (IED's). With firearms being readily available and a simple internet search on "how to build a bomb" reveals…..and I quote….."About 197,000,000 results (0.32 seconds)" the threat is here to stay.

Response

As a security professional based within New York City, I have witnessed extreme changes within law enforcement and the private sector first hand. The State of New York has made additions and modifications to the penal law by incorporating terror related crimes and related offenses. Included within various legislation, bills were introduced to provide immunity for civilians reporting a potential terror related tip.

New York State has also implemented the Office of Homeland Security, a division mirroring the federal DHS. Under this division, security directors from the private sector are given the opportunity to attend counterterrorist awareness training. Training courses-including, surveillance detection, emergency planning, weapons of mass destruction (WMD) recognition, active shooter countermeasures and other counterterrorist courses are conducted within the State training facility as well as host facilities throughout the region.

In addition, New York State has created the Enhanced Security Guard Program. This intense forty-hour class is designed to provide front-line private sector security officers with the knowledge and skill set necessary to recognize and report various terrorist tactics and methodologies. Certified instruction modules include historical perspectives, access control, patrol techniques, the incident command structure and emergency planning. The course is geared toward current threats, offered through regional instructors and, with certain restrictions, is tax deductible.

Shortly after September 11th, significant improvements were initiated on a local level. The New York City Police Department has made great strides in the counterterrorism and public/private cooperation arenas as well. Innovative prevention/deterrence programs created by this agency include task force based response to strategic and soft targets centered throughout the City in order to disrupt possible terrorist surveillance activities.

The cooperation with the private sector is emanated through the "Shield" program. This program is under the auspicious of the Department's Counterterrorism Bureau and includes threat briefings as well as a local business program to report potential terrorist related transactions.

Included within Shield's mission is to provide critical infrastructure training to private security directors. This localized training, conducted within the Department's Regional Infrastructure

Protection Center, provides both an overview and continuing training resource for security directors responsible for commercial property protection.

In addition, New York City has created the "Safe & Secure" training program. Working in conjunction with local union officials, this program offers front-line security officers, doormen and maintenance workers from both the residential and commercial sectors, training on how to recognize and report potential terrorist activity.

As evidenced with the current incidents and arrests throughout our country…undoubtedly the terrorist threat is here to stay. Jurisdictions, on the federal, state and local levels are responsible for the gathering of intelligence, identification of potential perpetrators and the arrest of criminals. The responsibility for being knowledgeable of current threats, identification of vulnerabilities and being the last line of defense…ours.

The Local Criminal

Yes….undoubtedly the terrorist threat is very real and here to stay. We, as property managers, Board members, superintendents, doormen and security professionals have the utmost duty to provide a safe environment for our residents, tenants and guests. However, although the chances of your building or facility experiencing a major terrorist attack maybe *possible*, the chances of your property being targeted by a local criminal is highly *probable*. These localized threats from the "common criminal" can take the form of a simple trespass on your property to a violent crime perpetrated against an individual.

We, as professionals mentioned above, are in a "responsible charge position". Weather implied by job title, employment scope or in a volunteer leadership role, have a *moral* obligation to offer protection to those who entrust us with their properties.

So…..imagine this scenario... you are in charge of a residential or commercial property. One of your tenants has just advised you that the lock on the front door of the building has been known to malfunction from "time-to-time". As a diligent professional, you have the maintenance crew inspect the lock.

The crew reports the lock seemed to stick occasionally, but has been oiled and now seems "OK". Three days later the same tenant advises you that the same lock has again been malfunctioning. This individual further advises they know there has been an increase in robberies within the neighborhood and they are becoming fearful. Again, you notify the maintenance staff. The maintenance personnel advise they are currently working on a flood emergency and will check the lock when finished. Upon the end of the workday, the crew decides they will check the lock "tomorrow".

Later that evening, your tenant arrives at the building. Entering through the front door, she abruptly interrupts a criminal attempting to break into a first floor unit. The perpetrator turns his attention from the unit and your tenant falls victim to a violent assault, robbery and is seriously and permanently injured...

Legal Obligation

In today's litigious times, the issue of liability is paramount. Courts nationwide have determined that failure to warn, maintain and/or correct situations within a premise are grounds for litigation.

Within the protection arena, successful litigation for a host of issues including inadequate security, negligent hiring, negligent retention, failure to train and failure to supervise, can result in large jury awards and have catastrophic consequences.

The national average for defending an action can well exceed $100,000.00 and the average cost for case settlement currently exceeds $500,000. Where cases have "gone the distance", jury verdicts average an award of $2,000,000. and have reached as high as $16,000,000. In addition to the monetary damages, the unquantifiable costs, including damage to corporate reputation, decreased confidence from investors, low employee/tenant morale and the potential for reduced occupancy levels can destroy a once prosperous and well respected organization.

When we consider premises liability from a protection standpoint, we must consider three legal parameters; Duty, Breach and Causation.

1. Duty: Did the owner/agent have a legal duty to protect the person? In a landmark case, Kline v. 1500 Mass Ave Apt Corp 1970, the court ruled the "Special Relationships Doctrine", once exclusively applied to the "innkeeper/guest", also applies to the landlord/tenant relationship. While on the property, the owner/agent must provide *reasonable* security precautions for all tenants and visitors. Please keep in mind that this does not mean the owner/agent must <u>guarantee</u> security. The reasonable care standard requires the owner/agent to provide protection adequate to <u>reasonably</u> counter the existing criminal threat.

2. Breach: Did the owner/agent violate the duty to protect? Did the owner/agent know or <u>should have</u> known there was a <u>probability</u> that the specific crime would occur? Was the criminal incident foreseeable? When we consider breach of duty and the foreseeability of crime we must consider three factors; Crime Demographics, Location of Premises and Organizational Nature.

A. Crime Demographics: Have there been any criminal incidents within the building, on the property, or within the surrounding neighborhood? Has there been a pattern of a specific type of crime? Statistical analysis plays a vital role in predicting criminal incidents within a neighborhood. Local police agencies are, of course, the best source for reported crime throughout your area. An additional source, which should be utilized, includes interviews and conversations with the local business establishments and residents in the neighborhood. This will provide you with a "feel" for the neighborhood and prove to be invaluable when considering unreported criminal incidents.

Statistical analysis and neighbor interviews should be conducted on a regular basis and include an assessment of neighborhood disarray (graffiti, dilapidated buildings, etc...).

B. Location of Premises: The physical location of the premise also plays a vital role in determining foreseeability of criminal incidents.

A location on a secluded street vs. a heavily traveled thoroughfare affects the propensity for a crime to occur. Another affecting factor is the evaluation of the economic demographics within the neighborhood. The U.S. Census Bureau plays a key role in this statistical analysis. Persons in charge of individual units within a building must also consider this parameter when evaluating security. Considerations of ground floor vs. upper floor, areas accessible to the general public vs. semi-private areas affect the foreseeability of crime and respective countermeasures.

C. Organizational Nature: Fact - shopping center parking lots have a criminal foreseeability for theft related crime. Fact - a nightclub with a young clientele has the foreseeability for assault related crime. Fact - at 3:00 AM, a convenience store with one clerk has the foreseeability of a robbery occurring. Certain premises, just by the nature of their business or demographics of their clientele, have the "automatic foreseeability" of certain crimes. Although your property may not contain one of these "automatic" premises, if it is within close proximity of one, you must address the probability of crime "spilling over" to your property and provide reasonable countermeasures.

3. Causation: Did the person suffer an injury or loss which was directly caused by the breach? Was the breach just a factor in the injury or loss? Courts have determined that either "cause in fact" (a direct cause) or "proximate cause" (a factor) are grounds for litigation.

As an owner or agent, if you had the duty to protect the person, failed to reasonably protect them and this failure was a cause of their injuries or loss, you may be held liable.

The Three Lessons

So....we know three things so far:

1. The terrorist and local criminal threat is absolutely here to stay.

2. We have a _moral_ obligation to provide protection for our residents, tenants and guests.

3. We have a _legal_ obligation to provide reasonable security measures adequate to counter those threats.

How We Do It

When we consider threats from the terrorist through the local street criminal there needs to be a process we can utilize to adequately and reasonably counter those threats within a cost effective and efficient manner. Of course, the type of technology and number of components will fluctuate, depending upon the threat itself, the profile of your particular building as well as other factors including the foreseeability of a certain crime occurring. In all cases, we need a systematic approach to protection.

In today's protection environment, more and more properties are installing security technology. In fact, closed circuit television, access control and intrusion detection systems are rapidly being deployed in every environment. These buildings, from the small three story walk-up residential building, to the sprawling college campus are installing various protective systems. Due to this rapid increase in security measures, we have seen the utilization of systems move from being a "luxury" to an absolute _standard of care_ throughout the United States.

So...how do we do it? First and foremost...start at the beginning.

The Vulnerability Assessment

Before any vendor is called in. Before any system design takes place. Before any thoughts of components are drafted. We need to take a hard look at what _has_ occurred or which _may_ occur within the property and develop an analytical approach to mitigate those threats.

When devising security plans to defend against threats, start at the beginning. In every protection scenario, the <u>neighborhood</u> in which your property is located has a direct impact on the strategy you utilize to protect your building.

Start with the "drive-by". Drive at least twenty blocks in each direction. Circle the neighborhood and pay close attention to the residences and commercial establishments that encompass your area. Note buildings that seem to be "falling apart" or otherwise appear in disarray. Buildings such as these tend to invite criminal attention.

Next, pay attention to recognized landmarks which could offer an opportunity for attack or protest. Consider scenarios that may affect your building should an incident occur. These collateral damage assessments are vital to ensure the security of your building.

Once your drive-by is complete, it's time to determine the crime rate within your community. The paramount resource for crime intelligence is the local law enforcement agency. In my immediate jurisdiction, it is the New York City Police Department. This agency maintains records on criminal incidents, including property theft and violent crime. Responsible persons should arrange an appointment with the precinct's Crime Prevention Officer. This professional can advise you of the specific criminal incidents which have occurred in your immediate area or "sector". In addition, current and emerging patterns of activity are tracked and analyzed. This information is of great importance when determining protection requirements for your specific building.

When determining the neighborhood crime rate, one important resource that should not be overlooked are the local residents and business establishments. Residents, owners and employees of area buildings and businesses should be consulted. These people are most likely aware of incidents which have occurred within their surrounding area, but not reported to the police. By consulting these individuals, you will not only have the official reported crime rate but a glimpse into activities not reported by crime victims.

The determination of a "low", "medium" or "high" crime rate, evaluation of the neighborhoods' overall "attitude" and collateral damage issues, all play a vital role in protection. The incorporation of your findings and knowledge of current threats, provide the backbone for a solid protection program.

Upon completion of the neighborhood assessment, it's time to begin a physical audit of your particular building. Look at the entire property from a would-be perpetrators state of mind. Start with the city streets surrounding your property. Ensure lighting fixtures are operational and properly maintained by the City authorities. Other considerations such as traffic flow and parking regulations, should be studied and an impact-analysis incorporated within your security audit.

Next, look at the exterior of your building. Ensure all signs of disarray, such as graffiti, are removed. Make certain all proprietary lighting systems are fully functional and properly illuminate the area. Lighting, when used correctly, will aid in deterring criminal activity.

Physical security systems, such as fencing, gates, doors and locks need to be constructed and installed in accordance with acceptable industry standards. Without applying these standards, your protective devices may not effectively secure your building. At the very minimum, all points of possible entry need protection. Ensure all existing hardware is in proper working order and repair, replace or upgrade as appropriate.

In addition, windows encompassing the building should be protected.   There are a variety of protection options available and depending upon your particular window configuration, may not involve a great deal of capital outlay.

The utilization of security technology, such as closed circuit television, access control and intrusion detection systems all play a vital role in protection. The installation and maintenance of a quality protection apparatus may involve substantial capital investment. In addition, the industry is rapidly featuring new and improved technology. Management personnel needs to thoroughly research available technologies and ensure the total system cost, including maintenance and monitoring, fall within their applicable budgets.

Once the exterior portion of your audit is complete, it's time for the internal inspection. It is advisable to start from the lowest floor and work upward.

Verify that all points addressed in the exterior portion carry over into the internal areas. For example, a lock employed on an exterior door has hardware that requires inspection on the interior side. Ensure all points of entry and exit are adequately protected.

After the physical security audit is complete, you have formed the essential framework for protection. Upon implementing realistic improvements, you have commenced construction of a quality security program.

Next within our vulnerability assessment we need to analyze our protection programs. These programs have been identified as the essential core of a quality defense plan. By incorporating clear-cut procedures with available technology, you will have the synergy necessary for protection. When implementing or managing security programs, consider the following:

Access Control: The fundamental reason for building security is to keep unauthorized persons out of your building. Depending upon the size and threat level of your building, access control processes range from a doorman, verifying identity through personal recognition, to the use of sophisticated biometric systems. In all cases, site-specific procedures should be implemented. Procedures should address remedies for unauthorized persons attempting access to - and found within the building.

Key Control: In order to maintain key control, you must first assess your existing process of issuance and retention. Begin by identifying critical areas of your building. Next, conduct an inventory of your current key and blank supply. Ensure all keys are accounted for and properly secured. Keys to perimeter door locks may be issued to residents and employees. Duplication prevention, should you have a "standard keying system", most likely, is not under your control. At

10

a minimum, critical areas of the building, such as electrical and telephone rooms as well as internal offices, will need a strict key issuance procedure and log. Replacement with a high-security keying system may be warranted if existing keys and blanks were lost or otherwise missing.

Communications: During an emergency situation, communication between staff, management and emergency responders is essential. Depending upon the size of the building and number of employees, the procurement of a portable radio system may be a wise investment. When making this decision, managers should be aware of maintenance costs. Replacement batteries and unit repairs need to be considered and incorporated within applicable budgets.

An alternative, usually reserved for a building with one or two employees, is the usage of personal cellular telephones. A simple verbal agreement, between management and staff, may provide a means for adequate communication in the event of an emergency. In either scenario, managers should be wary of potential "dead spots" within their properties. These "dead spots" disable communications and could be a potential hazard for employees responding to an incident.

Paperwork: Security logs are a crucial component of a quality protection program. By instituting and maintaining logs for alarm tests, package deliveries, criminal incidents and visitors, you will have a verifiable way of tracking the effectiveness of your security apparatus. In addition, you will be able to identify deficiencies and provide essential corrective action.

Access and key control, emergency communications and the necessary evil of paperwork, all have a vital role in protecting your residents, employees and guests from a variety of threats in today's uncertain times.

As we progress through our assessment, we come to a vital and pivotal point. Employees… the property's potential assets or disastrous liabilities.

As a manager, you are charged with the overall protection of your building. As a diligent manager, you have ensured all locks are working properly, alarms are installed and cameras are watching all

11

access points into your building. You know the doorperson or security officer is watching the cameras, monitoring the alarms and making sure all is protected. One question… _WHO_, in reality, is this person? Who did you entrust to hold the "keys to the castle"?

The old adage, "you never really know someone", may certainly be true, but by performing background investigations, you will have a glimpse into the character of a potential employee.

Start with the information the candidate has given you… the employment application. This vital document offers a wealth of information. The verification of the application is the first step of the investigation. Any "misstatements" by a potential employee is, of course, your first character indicator.

After the candidate passes the interview and application verification process, you're ready to proceed to the "next level". Before proceeding, ensure an appropriate release form has been signed. The release form should comply with current requirements of the Fair Credit Reporting Act. It is advisable to periodically consult legal counsel to ensure the release is current.

The investigation parameters should be consistent with the employment vacancy. Traditionally, managerial positions require a more comprehensive investigation.

At the very minimum, the investigation should encompass a verification of personal information, to include name and Social Security Number. A seven year residence, employment, criminal history, credit and driver's license check should be performed. Documentation will need to be cross-referenced. For example, during the course of the investigation it was determined that a candidate lived in Alabama, New Mexico and Idaho. A criminal history will need to encompass all applicable States. Imagine not including this within the investigation and it was determined the reason this candidate moved, was a violent criminal past.

Investigative services vary from the "do-it-yourself" internet-databases to professional, licensed, bonded and insured private investigative agencies. Depending upon budgetary constraints, you will

12

need to determine which option is suitable. Traditionally, internet-databases provide a means for the client to enter applicable information, attain pertinent records and conduct the assessment process themselves.

This avenue offers the manager a relatively inexpensive way to conduct background investigations. The alternative, the private investigator, can provide all required services and independently confirm the person indicated in documents is actually the candidate. In addition, the investigator can provide interpretation and valuable insight on conflicting documentation. This alternative, although customarily more expensive, provides an independent assessment of employment suitability.

People are indeed products of their past. By performing comprehensive background investigations, you are providing yet another degree of protection for your residents and reducing your corporate liability.

So far, we have covered the need for a neighborhood assessment, physical security audit, protective program management and employee background screening. The next phase of the assessment should be emergency procedures and training.

All emergency procedures should answer the six basic questions: who, what, where, when, why and how. In addition, you will need to establish a procedure for each threat to your building or facility. Do not forget incidents not related to security, such as fires, gas leaks, power losses and natural disasters.

Who? Determine who will respond. All crises will need an incident commander to instruct staff and deal with responding emergency services. The incident commander will need to be the senior ranking member of the building on duty at the time. Larger properties often have a security staff that is capable of responding to incidents. Smaller facilities and buildings may want to consider predetermined volunteers to aid in evacuation of residents and staff should the need arise.

What? Enact orders that will advise employees on what they are actually required to do. For example, one employee may be designated to call 911. Other employees may be assigned to search for suspicious items in and around public access ways.

Where? Ensure that responding employees know exactly where they are going and how to get there. Ensure your procedure does not include evacuation routes that pass through areas of the building that may create a safety hazard. You may also want to designate a command post for prolonged incidents. The command post should be located within proximity of the incident but far enough away to avoid hazards. The incident commander should be stationed within the command post with all necessary documents to include building floor plans and fire safety information.

When? The beginning of each procedure should be to call 911. You do not want to respond to incidents until you know help is on the way. Imagine missing this important step, for example, reacting to a report of a fire and the fire department doesn't respond because no one informed them. A simple indication to "Notify 911" should be paramount within the procedure. Only after notification should people respond.

Why? The inclusion of "why" in the emergency procedure addresses the specific outcome of the event. Phrases such as "render first-aid when applicable" and "to prevent panic and ensure residents are evacuated in a calm manner, remember to speak in a clear, calm and steady tone" tend to reinforce the reason for the response.

How? This question deals primarily with training and education issues. Although it may not be written into the procedure, this is the most important step.

Ask yourself these questions:

Does my staff know how to properly operate fire extinguishers?

Are employees properly prepared to handle a suspicious package delivered to the property?

What will the doorperson actually do if a bomb threat were telephoned?

What will I do if a suspicious person is loitering within the building and I cannot immediately call the police?

The answers to these questions lie within one word: training. Training for emergency situations cannot be overemphasized. It is necessary to train all applicable personnel. Small residential buildings, mid-sized commercial establishments and large campuses all have different and unique training needs. These training needs and in some cases, legal requirements, may be mandated by law, regulation or simply moral obligation. At a minimum, once all emergency procedures have been written and tested, onsite training should be conducted. Personnel, including security officers, maintenance workers, doorpersons and in unique circumstances, residents, need to participate in simulated exercises. By actually walking through procedures, step by step, responses to incidents can become second nature.

Please remember, a simple procedure with a systematic flow far out ways a lengthy one. The acronym "KISS" should always be employed during the writing process:

"Keep It Simple and Short"

Yes…the vulnerability assessment includes, to say the least, multiple parameters. Please note, the aforementioned items are only a touch of the true-to-life assessment. Our entire protection program should include a detailed layered approach. The layers of protection must include personnel, procedures, programs and physical security systems. The topic of this publication centers on the acquisition of protection technology and ways to avoid a nightmarish outcome. Only by conducting the assessment may we know the true scope of what systems we may employ to adequately and reasonably protect the properties we are responsible for. By just centering on the technology itself and missing vital parameters, for example, a program and procedural response for an access control system, we are shortchanging our entire protection program.

The Protection Specification

We have covered a multitude of issues surrounding the protection of our building, facility or complex. So far we have addressed some of the current threats, our obligations and a systematic way to identify vulnerabilities within our specific sites.

So, let's say our assessment has determined the need to install "new" and replace "existing" security technology. Specifically, for example, we found the need to *add* an access control system and *replace* the existing surveillance system.

Are we now ready to start calling in the contractors and get those protection systems installed?

NOPE!! Not yet. Sorry!

Our next step in the process is to create a *realistic* budget for the protection systems. The budget should include not only parameters necessary for the initial installation of the systems but should also include a five year plan for additions, modifications and repair of damaged components. Please note, when creating your budget and designing the protection system(s) it is paramount the adage of "do one...do all" stay within your mind. For example, if the building has two laundry rooms and you install a system in one, you must install it within the other. Should an incident occur within the unprotected one you may be held liable under the "foreseeability" arena as previously discussed.

CAUTION: When determining your budgetary constraints it is absolutely, positively *VITAL* to include parameters *outside* the scope of the security systems. Miss this important step and your well crafted budget may very well be blown to Pluto.

Items of concern include, but aren't limited to the following:

1. Elevators: Historically, elevators are serviced and maintained by outside contractors. These contractors are responsible for the inner workings of the cabs, shafts and cabling within the elevators.

In order to install protection components within the elevators there must be electrical power and cabling capable of transmitting a signal. The signal may include a video image, authorized "keyfob swipe" or alarm indication.

Typically, the elevator contractor will install and provide the necessary components within their prevue for use by security contractors. This cost must be included within the security budget. It is important to note, should the security personnel install these on their own, the elevator service agreement in place may be voided. Of course, a nightmare scenario will be the security contractor installing their systems and shorting the electrical system or damaging the elevator components.

2. Labor: To utilize union or non-union labor must be decided upon before we move further into the process. Historically, the cost of unionized contractors have proven to be significantly higher than their non-union counterparts. In addition, certain locations may require a "prevailing wage" rate be paid to employees as a matter of law.

3. Electrical Connectivity: All protection system components must have electrical power in order to operate. The decision must be made to have the necessary power components installed by in-house proprietary employees, by an outsourced electrical contractor or have the awarded contractor install the required devices. Either way it is accomplished, the connectivity will have an impact on the protection budget.

4. Insurance Bonds: The requirement for a performance and/or payment bond for the project must be decided when creating the budget. Typically, larger projects should require a performance bond to ensure the awarded contractor completes the installation professionally and within the scope of work. In addition, in order to ensure subcontractors are paid and do not walk off the job, which will absolutely delay the project, the issuance of a payment bond should be considered.

5. Plaster, Patch and Repair: Installations may require drilling or modifying physical components of the building.

The mandatory requirement of correcting these situations by repairing and plastering ceilings and walls or patching up and repainting drill holes will certainly add to your budget.

Next, once we have a firm budget in place, we need to create a plan of action to present to the *potential* contractors. This "Specification" is a vital step and necessary for organizations to provide proposals for the installation. The Specification also protects against miscommunications and ensures everyone is on the same page throughout the process. This vital document also demonstrates what is expected from the contractor from the pre-installation meeting to final system tests.

Our plan needs to address the same basic questions of Who? What? Where? When? Why? and How? By answering these questions we will form the virtual framework necessary for our project.

Our Specification should be divided into sections with each one clearly defining the task at hand. Using our example of installing a new access control system and replacing an existing surveillance system, our document should include the following components:

1. Cover Page: The cover page identifies the entity who is soliciting the proposals, the title of the project, the solicitation number, the primary physical location of the installation and date of document release.

2. Table of Contents: A clear and concise TOC should immediately follow our cover page. This will prove to be invaluable when referencing certain components within the document.

3. Individual Sections: The compartmentalization of the document will provide an organized approach to the entire request for proposals (RFP) process. The following sections, according to our example, may mirror the following pages.

A. Section One: Project Overview: This part of the document should include necessary contact information, project site identification, building descriptions as well as solicitation particulars such as walkthrough appointments and proposal deadlines. The following offers an example of this section:

PROJECT OVERVIEW

PROJECT MANAGEMENT:	Criminal Intelligence Administration
MAILING ADDRESS:	38-11 Ditmars Boulevard
	Astoria, New York 11105
TELEPHONE:	718.541.0723
FACSIMILE:	718.504.7530
EMAIL:	ceo@protect.nyc
CONTACT:	Timothy M. O'Brien, CPP

SITE IDENTIFICATION:	XYZ Corporation
PHYSICAL LOCATION:	XXXX East Anywhere Avenue
	Any Town, State 12345

DESCRIPTION: XYZ Corporation has been identified as eight high-rise residential buildings resting on approximately nineteen acres of land. The property was placed in service in 1961 and is a not-for-profit housing company, originally organized under the Limited Profit Housing Companies Act and falls under the auspices of the New York City Department of Housing Preservation and Development.

The property boundaries are identified as XXX Street to the North, XXX Street to the South, YYY Boulevard to the West and ZZZ Drive to the East. The eight (8) residential buildings have been identified as containing 3,873 residential units, professional suites, laundry facilities and eight (8) passenger elevators. The buildings are constructed primarily of brick masonry with glazing contained within the lobby areas and individual residential units throughout the perimeter.

The exterior portion of the property encompasses a swimming complex, outdoor sitting areas and an active children's playground. In addition, also under the control of property management are five (5) residential parking lots.

The commercial area has been identified as having four (4) retail units and no commercial parking lots. Furthermore, the property also contains a fully functioning boiler plant. This plant generates heat and hot water for the entire property.

SOLICITATION ISSUED:	Friday, February 2, 20xx	@ 9:00 AM
SITE WALK-THROUGH:	Monday, February 20, 20xx	@ Noon
PROPOSAL DEADLINE:	Friday March 15, 20xx	@ 5:00 PM
MAILING ADDRESS (1):	XYZ Corporation	
	XXXX East Anywhere Avenue	
	Any Town, State 12345	
	Attn: Joe Shmoe	

MAILING ADDRESS (2):	**Criminal Intelligence Administration**
	38-11 Ditmars Boulevard
	Astoria, New York 11105
	Attn: Timothy M. O'Brien, CPP

NOTE 1: Each location must receive one (1) original proposal and two (2) identical copies.

NOTE 2: All proposals must be received by the deadline in order to be considered.

Project Description: The Criminal Intelligence Administration has been appointed Project Manager for the complete installation of an integrated digital imaging and access control system.

The digital imaging portion of the project encompasses the installation of forty-eight (48) fixed interior surveillance cameras, two (2) exterior fixed surveillance cameras, eighteen (18) exterior PTZ cameras, fourteen (14) monitors, seven (7) digital video recorders and one (1) operational monitoring station within the Security Command Center.

The access control portion of the project involves the installation of ten (10) proximity readers for the residential buildings and eight (8) readers for the residential parking control gates. All installed access control readers, components and software will be integrated with the aforementioned surveillance apparatus and existing parking lot protective hardware.

B. Section Two: Digital Imaging System: This component and subsequent sections involve the specifying of the systems to be installed. In our example, we are replacing the current surveillance system and adding a new access control system. The items within this section are included as a reference only and parts are offered as an example of a technical based specification.

DIGITAL IMAGING SYSTEM

(Sample Overview of Project)

The digital imaging system installation plan includes the installation of surveillance devices within the interior and exterior of the eight (8) residential buildings. The installation process involves the complete compartmentalization of the surveillance systems. Each residential building will act as an independent system. The compartmentalization will eliminate the need for hard-wire runs throughout the property, with the exception of the tri-level parking garage. Each unit (building) will have the capability of acting as an independent surveillance center. The installation plan includes the utilization of a Digital Subscriber Line (DSL) and/or cable modem hardwired within the units digital video recorders. A central monitoring station will be located within the Security Command Center and all live images will be viewable via surveillance monitors.

This portion of the project encompasses the installation of forty-eight (48) fixed interior surveillance cameras, two (2) exterior fixed surveillance cameras, eighteen (18) exterior PTZ cameras, fourteen (14) monitors, seven (7) digital video recorders and one (1) operational monitoring station within the Security Command Center.

SUBSECTION A: Residential Building Identification

The following addresses encompass the residential portion of XYZ Corporation:

NUMBER	ADDRESS	STORIES
ONE	XXX Boulevard	21
TWO	XXX Boulevard	21
THREE	XXX West Any Street	21

FOUR	*XXX West Any Street*	*21*
FIVE	*XXX Avenue*	*21*
SIX	*XXX Avenue*	*21*
SEVEN	*XXX Drive*	*22*
EIGHT	*XXX Road*	*38*

SUBSECTION B: Residential Parking Lot Identification

The following locations encompass the residential parking lots of XYZ Corporation:

NUMBER	LOCATION	SPACES
R-1	*R/O XXX Boulevard*	*321*
R-2	*R/O XXX Boulevard*	*388*
R-3	*F/O XXX West Any Street*	*421*
R-4	*F/O XXX West Any Street*	*88*
R-5	*S/O XXX Avenue*	*952*

(Samples/Portions of Technical Camera Requirements)

SUBSECTION C: Installation Parameters – Surveillance Cameras

1. The fifty (50) surveillance cameras for this phase shall consist of fixed high resolution color dome cameras. The following minimum specifications shall be consistent with the proposal:

- *The camera shall have the form factor as typical of a CCTV dome video camera.*

- *The image capturing device shall be a 1/3-inch interline transfer super HAD CCD image sensor.*

- *The camera shall have digital signal processing.*

- *The camera shall have automatic backlight compensation.*

2. The eighteen (18) exterior PTZ surveillance cameras shall consist of high resolution day/night dome cameras. The following minimum specifications shall be consistent with the proposal:

- *The unit shall use direct drive technology for smooth movement. No gears or belts shall be used in the drive system.*

- *The system shall use closed-loop positioning technology.*

- *Preset positioning accuracy shall be within ±0.015 degrees.*

SUBSECTION D: Surveillance Camera Installations

I. Building Identification: XXX Boulevard

CAMERA NUMBER: I-38-001

CAMERA LOCATION: Outer Lobby Vestibule

TYPE OF INSTALLATION: New - Fixed Interior

This surveillance point shall conform to the aforementioned specifications. This dome camera will be permanently mounted to the interior ceiling. The field of view shall be the outer lobby vestibule and include images of individuals accessing the door.

This section will usually include additional technical specifications to include power requirements, transmission media as well as requirements for the recorders and monitors.

Each subsequent section, for example, Section Three: Access Control System and Section Four: The Security Command Center (if applicable), will yield the same format and include component locations as well as system specific requirements.

Readers are encouraged to either seek the aid of an independent consultant, or should you choose to issue the solicitation in-house, may wish to eliminate the technical aspects of the specification. In either case, this publication discusses some of the more common pitfalls associated with selecting the wrong vendor.

The Request for Proposals (RFP)

So, now we have determined our threats, met our obligations, systematically identified our vulnerabilities, carefully crafted our budget and wrote a specification to present to our potential contractors. Now it's time to create our Request for Proposals. Generally speaking, the more information we receive from a potential contractor during this process, the better. Our solicited information may save us from possible headaches after award. Throughout the following pages we will see potential nightmares begin to unfold....

The RFP document is utilized to form a standard proposal format which answers all the questions from vendor pedigree information through each component of the system and ending with costs associated with the entire installation. Traditionally, the document is included as a section within our specification. Using our example, let us call this: Section Five: Proposal Parameters

Our first page within this section should provide the summary of technology for the project. An example of this summary may look similar to the following:

PROPOSAL PARAMETERS

The Criminal Intelligence Administration, in concert with XYZ Corporation, is seeking a qualified contractor to provide installation services as outlined within the preceding specification document. The selected contractor will be responsible for providing all outlined services, to include fully installed and operational systems, electrical connections, plaster and painting. In addition to organization-specific proposals, the enclosed Residential Protection Proposal will need to be submitted. This form, requested attachments, manufactures specification sheets and your organizations' proprietary proposal, will need to be submitted in order to be considered.

1. Specification Summary:

LOCATION	SYSTEM COMPONENTS	TOTALS
RESIDENTIAL BUILDINGS - INTERIOR	SURVEILLANCE CAMERAS	48
EXTERIOR OF BUILDINGS - FIXED	SURVEILLANCE CAMERAS	2
RESIDENTIAL BUILDINGS - PTZ	SURVEILLANCE CAMERAS	14
PARKING FACILITIES - INTERIOR-FIXED	SURVEILLANCE CAMERAS	N/A
PARKING FACILITIES - PTZ	SURVEILLANCE CAMERAS	4
RESIDENTIAL SECURITY DESKS	SURVEILLANCE MONITORS	14
OPERATIONS CENTER	SURVEILLANCE MONITORS	8
XYZ CORPORATION	DIGITAL VIDEO RECORDERS	7
RESIDENTIAL BUILDINGS	ACCESS CONTROL READERS	10
PARKING FACILITIES	ACCESS CONTROL READERS	8
XYZ CORPORATION	INITIAL SUPPLY/KEYFOBS	6,000

The actual RFP, which we will call the "Residential Protection Proposal", can either be bound within the section or attached separately to the specification. Either way, the following will need to be included within the document:

1. Project Identification: This portion includes the name of the entity who is soliciting the proposals, the solicitation number, the primary physical location of the installation, date of document release and the deadline for proposals.

2. Contractor Pedigree, Contact and Policies: This part identifies the "legal" entity who is proposing services and all the basic information regarding that entity. Included within this portion should be the following:

A. Legal Business Name: The actual *legal* name of the entity needs to be known. Many companies will utilize a "DBA" (Doing Business As) and not the legal corporate name.

Potential Pitfall: Imagine you are awarding a new contract and during your due diligence you conduct a search for any pending lawsuits against your potential contractor, "<u>Made-Up</u> Company Protection". The search revealed negative results and you proceed to award. However, the contractor's legal company name is "<u>My Real Company</u> Protection" and has multiple lawsuits pending for providing substandard protection equipment. Yes…potential nightmare.

Just for the record…the potential pitfalls and examples contained throughout this publication are <u>actual</u> events witnessed throughout my thirty-plus years within the protection industry. Although the examples are real, any and all references to entities described within the examples and pitfalls are fictional.

B. Contact Information: This portion should include the corporate address (not just the local branch office), applicable telephone/facsimile numbers, email addresses, website and contact persons (including titles).

C. Credit and Regulatory Information: Applicable State and local license numbers, Employer Identification Numbers (EIN), Dun & Bradstreet identifyers, CAGE Codes (for US Government contracts) and State/year of incorporation along with registration numbers should all be included within the document.

Potential Pitfall: Please ensure all potential contractors are licensed within the jurisdiction of the project. In addition, ensure they have been incorporated within the jurisdiction for no less than five years and have applicable credit history.

So, here we go. A residential management firm hired a contractor to install a surveillance system within a large sprawling apartment complex.

The contractor accepted the _large deposit_ for the project and installed a few cameras, recorders and monitors. After a week the contractor's presence on the property became scarce. Then, by the third week...poof! Yes...he disappeared with the deposit and walked-off the installation.

No, he wasn't licensed by the State. No, he had no confirmed credit history. Yes! He was incorporated...but only for one year.

...and yes, a nightmare.

D. Parent Company Parameter: The question of "Do you have a parent company?" should always be asked during the RFP process. This will ensure you know exactly "who" you are hiring.

Potential Pitfall: Stop me if you've heard this one...a commercial property management firm needs to award a high-value protection contract. So, being ever so diligent they invite twenty contractors to submit proposals for the project. The firm uses their process and narrows the field down to four contenders. Let's call them Company A, Company B, Company C and Company D. Well, the management firm never asked the "parent company" question. Turns out, companies "A", "C" and "D" were wholly owned subsidiaries of one of the other entities that failed to make the final cut.

Talk about stacking the deck.....

E. Prior Company Name: This component asks if the contractor has ever changed the company name within the last seven years.

Although I could probably write three pages just on this one...I'll leave it with one question...

What if the reason the company changed its name was because the prior name had a horrific reputation in the industry, lost multiple lawsuits for negligence and never paid subcontractors for work they performed?

Yup...enough said.

F. Public Filings: Questions that should always be asked of an organization include:

1. Has the corporation filed for bankruptcy protection within the past five years?

2. Has the corporation ever been found guilty of a criminal act?

Potential Pitfall: Imagine awarding a contractor a project and they have a bankruptcy pending? Where will they get the components for the project? Did they list their suppliers as debts they can't pay? Will other suppliers grant them credit for the cameras, recorders and monitors for your project? Will subcontractors work for them and get paid? Is your potential contractor submitting a proposal and worrying about the above questions *after* they get the award and deposit?

Another scenario, did the company get fined or receive criminal violations for not complying with licensing requirements? Did those violations include gross negligent or intentional acts?

All of course...nightmare scenarios.

G. Corporate Integrity: A couple of questions that may be asked of the company involve background investigations of employees, corporate drug and alcohol policies and if the company bonds their employees. The answers to these questions gives you an overall sense of the integrity of the entity.

H. Insurance & Bonding Levels: In the beginning of the process, before a contractor is even considered a contender, the questions regarding insurance and bonding (if required) levels should be addressed.

Potential Pitfall: So, you've just went through an exhaustive RFP process, selected your installation company and FINALLY signed a contract.

Houston.....we have a problem. The contractor can't make your minimum insurance requirements.

Reset button pressed.....do over called!

I. Subcontractors: A great majority of entities within the protection arena decide to subcontract portions of an installation project. Traditionally, the pre-wiring of buildings and in some cases, the mounting of system components are outsourced. Larger companies provide what is called, "smarts and parts". This term is used when the "prime contractor" provides all the necessary system components and relies on the subcontractor to wire and install them. Upon installation, the prime returns with proprietary employees and provides the "smarts", which is programing, troubleshooting and testing.

Another scenario involves utilizing a subcontractor for a complete turnkey installation. This process has the subcontractor acquire all components, wire the building, install the equipment and perform programing and testing. A modified version exists where the prime supplies only the system components.

Potential Pitfall: The utilization of subcontractors may present a potential disaster. After thorough research and careful consideration, you have awarded the contract to an entity who has met all of your requirements. But.....wait. Who are these people on your project?

Unless you specifically ask if the awarded contractor will utilize a subcontractor, historically, this information will not be volunteered. Why? Simply because divulging such information may yield a host of questions. Specifically, all of the questions that we asked the selected contractor *MUST* be asked of any subcontractors.

Imagine this scenario. A decision was made to hire ABC Protection. They have met all of your requirements and conform to your strict standards. They responded to all of your inquiries and passed with flying colors. Yes, they will have the ultimate responsibility for the completion of your project.

However, after the installation is underway you are feeling a little uneasy. Maybe you can't put your finger on it….but just uneasy. So, you decide to ask a few questions. The answers make you realize what it is….

The subcontractor was actually one of the potential prime contractors who bid on your project! They didn't get the project, although they were the cheapest, because they aren't licensed, had multiple lawsuits, have a horrific reputation and never conducted background checks! Oh wait….no background checks? Who are these people on my property? Are they criminals? Maybe career criminals?

I'll just leave it at that and let you think…

No, I won't. There is actually another problem. The contractor that was awarded the project may have conspired with this vendor to enhance both of their chances at award. So much for passing the integrity test.

True story…this happened.

So, back to our Residential Protection Proposal. The following pages illustrate a sample format of the form based on what we have covered so far:

CRIMINAL INTELLIGENCE ADMINISTRATION
38-11 Ditmars Boulevard ▪ Astoria, New York 11105
Telephone: 718.541.0723 ▪ Toll Free: 800.792.7181 ▪ Facsimile: 718.504.7530
Email: ceo@protect.nyc   www.protect.nyc

RESIDENTIAL PROTECTION PROPOSAL

Solicitation Identification:	RFP-00000000-R/O
Site Identification:	XYZ Corporation
Physical Location:	XXXX East Anywhere Avenue
	Any Town, State 12345
Solicitation Issued:	February 2, 20xx @ 9:00 AM
Proposal Deadline:	March 15, 20xx @ 5:00 PM

LEGAL BUSINESS NAME _____ D/B/A _____

CORPORATE ADDRESS _____ CITY _____ STATE _____ ZIP _____

TELEPHONE _____ FACSIMILE _____ WEBSITE _____

CONTACT PERSON _____ TITLE _____ TELEPHONE _____ EMAIL ADDRESS _____

CORPORATE PRESIDENT _____ TELEPHONE _____ EMAIL ADDRESS _____

DUNS NUMBER(S) _____ CAGE CODE _____ EIN _____ NYS DOS LICENSE NUMBER _____ EXPIRATION _____

STATE OF INCORPORATION _____ YEAR _____ PRIOR CORPORATE NAME (IF CHANGED WITHIN THE PRECEDING SEVEN YEARS)

PARENT COMPANY (IF ANY) _____ CORPORATE ADDRESS _____ CITY _____ STATE _____ ZIP _____

TELEPHONE _____ FACSIMILE _____ WEBSITE _____

HAS THE CORPORATION FILED FOR BANKRUPTCY PROTECTION WITHIN THE LAST 5 YEARS?   Y ☐   N ☐

HAS THE CORPORATION EVER BEEN FOUND GUILTY OF A CRIMINAL ACT?   Y ☐   N ☐

DOES THE CORPORATION CONDUCT PRE-EMPLOYMENT BACKGROUND INVESTIGATIONS?   Y ☐   N ☐
☐ 7 YEAR CRIMINAL HISTORY   ☐ RESIDENCE VERIFICATION   ☐ CREDIT CHECK
☐ DMV LICENSE CHECK   ☐ SSN VERIFICATION   ☐ REFERENCE CHECK

OTHER(S) _____

DOES THE COMPANY HAVE A DRUG AND ALCOHOL POLICY IN EFFECT?   Y ☐ N ☐

ARE COMPANY EMPLOYEES BONDED? Y ☐ N ☐ WILL BONDED EMPLOYEES WORK ON THIS PROJECT? Y ☐ N ☐

BONDING COMPANY _____ ADDRESS _____ CITY _____ STATE _____ ZIP _____

TELEPHONE _____ FACSIMILE _____ WEBSITE _____

CONTACT PERSON _____ TITLE _____ TELEPHONE _____ EMAIL ADDRESS _____

DOES THE CORPORATION HAVE THE ABILITY TO ACQUIRE A PERFORMANCE BOND FOR THIS PROJECT? Y ☐ N ☐

IF SO, WHAT IS THE CURRENT BONDING LEVEL OF THE CORPORATION? $ _____

BONDING COMPANY	ADDRESS	CITY	STATE	ZIP

TELEPHONE	FACSIMILE	WEBSITE

CONTACT PERSON	TITLE	TELEPHONE	EMAIL ADDRESS

CORPORATE ENTITIES PERFORMING WORK WITHIN XYZ CORPORATION WILL NEED TO MAINTAIN, IN FULL FORCE AND EFFECT, ACTIVE INSURANCE POLICIES FOR THE DURATION OF THE PROJECT AND ANY EXTENSIONS AS PER SERVICE AGREEMENTS. THE POLICIES WILL NEED TO INCLUDE COMPREHENSIVE GENERAL LIABILITY AND AUTOMOBILE LIABILITY INSURANCE IN THE AMOUNT OF NOT LESS THAN $5,000,000. (FIVE MILLION USD) PER OCCURRENCE. IN ADDITION, CONTRACTORS WILL ALSO BE REQUIRED TO MAINTAIN ACTIVE WORKERS COMPENSATION AND DISABILITY INSURANCE POLICIES FOR THEIR EMPLOYEES PERFORMING WORK WITHIN THE BUILDINGS. ALL POLICIES SHOULD NOT BE SUBJECT TO CANCELLATION, NON-RENEWAL, REDUCTION IN POLICY TERMS OR OTHERWISE CHANGE IN COVERAGE FOR THE DURATION OF THE CONTRACT. APPLICABLE POLICIES WILL NEED TO INCLUDE XXXXX, INCORPORATED AND OTHERS, AS MAY BE REQUIRED, AS ADDITIONAL INSURED.

DOES YOUR ORGANIZATION HAVE INSURANCE POLICIES IN EFFECT AS PER THE ABOVE GUIDELINES?   Y ☐ N ☐

INSURANCE COMPANY	ADDRESS	CITY	STATE	ZIP

TELEPHONE	FACSIMILE	WEBSITE

CONTACT PERSON	TITLE	TELEPHONE	EMAIL ADDRESS

** ATTACHMENT REQUIRED – CERTIFICATE OF INSURANCE **

DOES THE CORPORATION INTEND TO ENTER INTO SUBCONTRACTING AGREEMENTS WITH OTHER INDIVIDUALS OR BUSINESS ENTITIES FOR THE PURPOSE OF COMPLETING THE PROJECT?   Y ☐   N ☐

IF YES, SUBCONTRACTORS WILL BE BOUND BY REQUIREMENTS AND PARAMETERS CONTAINED WITHIN THIS DOCUMENT.

SUBCONTRACTOR 1: PORTION OF PROJECT_____

LEGAL BUSINESS NAME	D/B/A

CORPORATE ADDRESS	CITY	STATE	ZIP

TELEPHONE	FACSIMILE	WEBSITE

CONTACT PERSON	TITLE	TELEPHONE	EMAIL ADDRESS	

DUNS NUMBER(S)	CAGE CODE	EIN	NYS DOS LICENSE NUMBER	EXPIRATION

STATE OF INCORPORATION	YEAR	PRIOR CORPORATE NAME (IF CHANGED WITHIN THE PRECEDING SEVEN YEARS)

PARENT COMPANY (IF ANY)	CORPORATE ADDRESS	CITY	STATE	ZIP

TELEPHONE	FACSIMILE	WEBSITE

HAS THE CORPORATION FILED FOR BANKRUPTCY PROTECTION WITHIN THE LAST 5 YEARS? Y ☐ N ☐

HAS THE CORPORATION EVER BEEN FOUND GUILTY OF A CRIMINAL ACT? Y ☐ N ☐

DOES THE CORPORATION CONDUCT PRE-EMPLOYMENT BACKGROUND INVESTIGATIONS? Y ☐ N ☐
☐ 7 YEAR CRIMINAL HISTORY   ☐ RESIDENCE VERIFICATION   ☐ CREDIT CHECK
☐ DMV LICENSE CHECK   ☐ SSN VERIFICATION   ☐ REFERENCE CHECK

OTHER(S) _____

DOES THE COMPANY HAVE A DRUG AND ALCOHOL POLICY IN EFFECT? Y ☐ N ☐

ARE COMPANY EMPLOYEES BONDED? Y ☐ N ☐ WILL BONDED EMPLOYEES WORK ON THIS PROJECT? Y ☐ N ☐

DOES THIS ORGANIZATION HAVE INSURANCE POLICIES IN EFFECT AS PER THE GUIDELINES? Y ☐ N ☐

INSURANCE COMPANY	ADDRESS	CITY	STATE	ZIP

TELEPHONE	FACSIMILE	WEBSITE

CONTACT PERSON	TITLE	TELEPHONE	EMAIL ADDRESS

Please note, protection companies may utilize multiple subcontractors for different elements of the project. It is important to duplicate the subcontractor portion of the document (I usually include five pages) in order for them to accurately report their use. In addition, when submitting the RFP document it is paramount that _all_ pages be returned. This includes the subcontractor pages. Should an entity not utilize portions of the RFP form they will need to indicate a "none" or "N/A" response.

3. Assigned Personnel: The document will need to include how many people will be assigned to this project. In addition, the utilization of union vs. non-union labor usually will be addressed within this section. The following offers an example of requirements:

```
THIS PROJECT WILL REQUIRE MULTIPLE WORK CREWS CONCURRENTLY WORKING ON ALL PORTIONS OF THIS
PROJECT. HOW MANY WORK CREWS WILL BE ASSIGNED TO THE FOLLOWING PORTIONS?

1. DIGITAL IMAGING SYSTEM          _____WORK CREWS_____TOTAL PERSONS/CREW_____SUPERVISORS

2. ACCESS CONTROL SYSTEM           _____WORK CREWS_____TOTAL PERSONS/CREW_____SUPERVISORS


THIS PROJECT DOES NOT SPECIFY MANDATORY UNION LABOR. IN ORDER TO ASSESS THE COST PARAMETERS OF
YOUR PROPOSAL, PLEASE INDICATE ONE OF THE FOLLOWING:

             ☐   OUR ORGANIZATION WILL ONLY UTILIZE UNION LABOR FOR THIS PROJECT

             ☐   OUR ORGANIZATION WILL UTILIZE NON-UNION LABOR


THIS PROJECT WILL ALSO REQUIRE AN ON-SITE INSTALLATION MANAGER TO ENSURE A SEAMLESS
INSTALLATION.

NAME OF PROPOSED INSTALLATION MANAGER (IF AVAILABLE DURING RFP)_____
```

Potential Pitfall: Take a real good look at this section of the RFP. There are just a few lines to read and ultimately to fill in. However, this is one of the most important elements of the proposal for your evaluation and consideration. Let's consider an example and yes…this is also one that actually happened:

Our "victim" in this example was an independent owner/manager of fourteen independent residential buildings situated within close proximity to one another. The project was to install surveillance cameras, recorders and monitors. Another parameter of the project involved integrating an access control system. Several vendors were solicited and the search was narrowed down to two potential candidates. Both companies proposed to install relatively similar components and utilize the same type of labor.

Now, My Camera Company, Inc. proposed a total of $78,000 (approximate) for the complete project installation.

I'm The Other Guy, Inc. proposed $84,000 (approximate) for their system.

......and the winner was?!?

My Camera Company, Inc. Why? Because they were less expensive and offered similar technology. Unfortunately, our "victim" in this case never asked how many work crews/technicians were proposed. As it turns out, there was only one person assigned to the project and it lasted well over a year.

One important and sad note, the components that were installed only had a manufacturer's warrantee for one year. The time it took the technician to complete the project....the warrantee expired. This element we will cover a little later in this publication.

4. Authorized Manufacturer Representative: The manufactures of protection technology require companies who install their systems to be authorized to do so. In addition, these entities also require training for technicians in order to be certified installers of their components. This should be a *mandatory* requirement for successful award of a protection contract.

Potential Pitfall: So, a contractor was awarded a contract for the installation of a well-known surveillance system. The monetary element of the contract was substantial and involved multiple site installations that were undergoing renovations. The contractor received their timely deposit, attended the onsite construction meetings and all was perfect in the beginning. Well, as the installation progressed certain elements of the system wouldn't work properly. The contractor needed help and there was a dire need to call the manufacture's support center. One problem....they weren't authorized to install the system. In addition, the technician did not have an individual passcode to access the support network. Needless to say, the project dragged on and not only delayed the protection end but ultimately delayed the completion of construction.

5. Lead/Completion Time Frames: The lead time for a contractor to mobilize should be known from the beginning. This should be committed in writing within the RFP form. Historically, smaller companies will require a longer lead time which may result in project delays. In addition, should the protection project coincide with construction schedules the entire project, as shown in our previous case, could be delayed. At this phase of the process, a timeframe for the complete installation of the systems should be included. This parameter may be estimated, however, as we will see further into the process, upon contract it will be binding.

6. Protection System Components: As we move further within our RFP document, we are now at the point of asking the potential contractor to enumerate the specific technology they are proposing. Each and every component will need to be itemized as per the following example:

1. DIGITAL IMAGING SYSTEM

A. INTERIOR SURVEILLANCE CAMERAS

MANUFACTURER	MODEL NUMBER	DESCRIPTION	UNINSTALLED UNIT COST

B. EXTERIOR SURVEILLANCE CAMERAS

MANUFACTURER	MODEL NUMBER	DESCRIPTION	UNINSTALLED UNIT COST

C. DIGITAL VIDEO RECORDERS

MANUFACTURER	MODEL NUMBER	DESCRIPTION	UNINSTALLED UNIT COST

D. MONITORING EQUIPMENT

MANUFACTURER	MODEL NUMBER	DESCRIPTION	UNINSTALLED UNIT COST

As we see in our very brief example, we want to know the specific manufacturer, model number, brief description and uninstalled unit cost for each and every component of the protection system.

Potential Pitfall (1): BUYER BEWARE! The protection industry has grown exponentially throughout recent years. Currently, there are well over a thousand manufactures of security technology. Components, such as cameras, digital video recorders, access control panels and card readers are being manufactured both within the local and international arenas. This rise in proprietary technology creates a unique and potentially disastrous problem.

So….here we go again:

A commercial high-rise awarded a seven figure installation contract for surveillance, access control and intrusion detection to the "lowest qualified bidder". The company conducted their due diligence on the background and credit worthiness of the contractor. All checked out OK and the project was completed without a hitch.

Four months after the installation various components started to fail. In the beginning the installing contractor repaired the components in a timely manner. As a few more months passed it became harder and harder to reach the contractor. After about a year, the contractor met with his customer and explained….the manufacturer of the components was located overseas and has since went out of business.

Guess what? Because the installer bought system components from a small company who manufactured their *own* proprietary systems there was no way to buy replacement parts. The entire system would have to be replaced!

Yes…the Yugo of security systems.

Now for the kicker…management had no legal recourse against the installer. Why? The installing company provided the manufacturer specification sheets and applicable information within their proposal. The proposal was accepted and signed off by management.

Another potential nightmare when buying proprietary technology involves your installing contractor and not the manufacturer. What happens if your contractor is the only representative on the East Coast, the Midwest or the United States? What if they go out of business and no other installer can access the components? What happens if they start charging you outrageous prices for service calls? Oh boy…

The moral of this story…only accept proposed components and systems from *nationally recognized manufacturers*. In addition, ensure the technology is available and offered to a wide selection of dealers through *industry recognized distributors* such as ADI and Anixter.

Potential Pitfall (2): Model & Description: Each manufacturer of protection technology offers variances of system components. Cameras, for example vary by size, shape, lens and offered features. It is imperative the exact model number and matching description be reveled within the proposal.

So, a residential building decided to install a surveillance system. They conducted all of the necessary contractor screening and awarded the project. The deposit check was cashed and all was progressing. As the installation moved forward and the contractor started to install the cameras….the HUGE, UGLY and GINORMOUS cameras, it became evident something wasn't quite right. When asked why the cameras weren't…let's say…aesthetically pleasing, he responded…these are the cameras we always install.

Oh no…CHANGE ORDER!

Potential Pitfall (3): **Uninstalled Unit Cost: The next portion of this section identifies the cost for each of the components. This very important piece of information will help alleviate headaches and "budgetaches" should the need arise to replace or add system technology.**

OK, during the course of a burglar alarm installation within a residential community the managing agent identified several key areas that required additional protection not included within the original Scope of Work. The very eager contractor provided another proposal for the additional components. WAIT! Why so much money for a few alarm contacts and motion detectors? The answer was simple. The contractor already had the job, the installation was well underway and he felt he can charge pretty much anything he wanted for additions. This of course is a shady business practice and eventually led to the demise of the contractors' business, but, it happened. By the way, this also applies to components that are vandalized or otherwise damaged by elements outside of normal wear and tear. Knowing the upfront cost of each component along with the avoidance of other pitfalls previously discussed will minimize the chances of a nightmarish outcome.

7. Installation Cost Breakdown: The total cost breakdown for any protection system should be included within the RFP document. The following is an example of this parameter:

INSTALLATION COSTS

ITEM DESCRIPTION	TOTAL INSTALLED COST
SURVEILLANCE SYSTEM COMPONENTS	$
MONITORING PANEL AND COMMAND COMPUTER	$
ELECTRICAL CONNECTIVITY/SURGE PROTECTION	$
PLASTER, PATCH AND REPAIR	$
DEBRIS REMOVAL	$
EMPLOYEE TRAINING	$
MISCELLANEOUS COSTS AND FEES	$
TOTAL INSTALLED SURVEILLANCE SYSTEM	$

8. Miscellaneous Fees & Expenses (Post-Installation): This parameter ensures any fees and expenses not associated with the initial installation are addressed before contract award.

This section should always be included and will prevent surprises and potential headaches long after the project is complete. The following illustrates this point:

Miscellaneous Fees & Expenses (Post Installation)

ITEM DESCRIPTION	TOTAL HOURLY COST
TECHNICAL ASSISTANCE (SOFTWARE)	$
GENERAL HOURLY BILL RATE FOR SERVICES	$

Potential Pitfall: **A well-known managing agent hired a contractor to install a security system within a residential high-rise building. Every portion of the project went smoothly and there were absolutely no residual issues. However, this important aspect of the RFP process was overlooked. As a matter of fact, there was no thought on how the five year plan would play out as we previously discussed in the budget section of this publication. So, what happened? The contractor historically charged customers $595. per hour for service calls with a four hour minimum. Needless to say, throughout the years this was a very expensive system to maintain.**

9. Manufactures Warrantee: This portion should address applicable warrantees offered for each component of the protection system. Typically, depending on the particular manufacturer, security systems have a one to five year warrantee period. The below illustrates a sample questionnaire:

DO INSTALLED COMPONENTS OFFER A MANUFACTURERS WARRANTEE? ☐ Y ☐ N

PLEASE INDICATE APPLICABLE WARRANTEE INFORMATION

SURVEILLANCE CAMERAS	_____ YEAR(S)	SYSTEM CABLES/WIRING	_____ YEAR(S)
DIGITAL VIDEO RECORDERS	_____ YEAR(S)	MONITORING EQUIPMENT	_____ YEAR(S)
MONITORING PANEL	_____ YEAR(S)	COMMAND COMPUTER	_____ YEAR(S)

ELECTRICAL CONNECTIVITY/SURGE PROTECTION   _____ YEAR(S)

10. Service/Maintenance Agreements: Upon the successful installation of the protection system a service/maintenance contract should be set into place. This agreement should address components which are in need of repair or replacement from normal wear and tear.

Items which are damaged via vandalism or by any other means, such as by flood or acts of god, are usually exempt from the agreement. Remember, these components will be covered under service calls and rates identified within the preceding portion (line item 8). This agreement should be effective on the day the system becomes operational and charges initiated after one year of continued service at no charge. The following example illustrates this portion of the RFP:

```
DOES YOUR ORGANIZATION OFFER AN ANNUAL SERVICE/MAINTENANCE PLAN?  ☐ Y  ☐ N

WHAT IS THE COST FOR AN ANNUAL AGREEMENT?  $_____P/YEAR

IS THERE A CANCELLATION CLAUSE?  ☐ Y  ☐ N

WHAT TIMEFRAME IS ALLOTTED FOR CANCELLATION ONCE THE AGREEMENT IS INITIATED?
_____

IF SYSTEM COMPONENTS FAIL AND NEED TO BE REMOVED FROM THE SITE, DO YOU HAVE LOANER
EQUIPMENT AVAILABLE UNTIL THE SYSTEM IS REPAIRED?  ☐ Y  ☐ N

ARE THERE ASSOCIATED COSTS WITH THE LOANER EQUIPMENT?  ☐ Y  ☐ N
```

Potential Pitfall (1): Be aware….be very aware of the responses to this question. Let me jump ahead for a second. During my RFP process, after all the proposals are submitted, opened and catalogued, there are two places I immediately look. The first is the total installed price and the second is the proposed service/maintenance agreement. Why? The primary reason is that within the protection industry there is a well-known phrase… "buying the job". This catchy little phrase could wreak havoc on your budget! The premise is simple. A contractor will offer a low installation price in anticipation of a high-priced annual service/maintenance agreement. Their thought pattern is they will be awarded the project and make more money over a five year span. The reality is that if another vendor were selected with a higher installation/lower service cost we would have saved a lot of money over the years. This attempted ploy is something I've seen more times than I care to remember.

Potential Pitfall (2): The Cancelation Clause: Ideally, the company who installed the system should be the one to maintain it throughout the years.

This happy marriage of sorts can and will prevent a host of problems from occurring. When we award a project we are looking for that happy relationship to continue with the selected contractor…well….actually….forever.

There are multiple issues surrounding the "takeover" of a system installed by another company. The first thing you will hear from a contractor entering the site post-installation is "Well, we didn't put the system in". This will be followed by "I really can't be sure what's wrong just by looking at it" and then finally the dreaded time and materials pitch. Oh no…T&M. There goes the budget.

By the way, do you know what the most dreaded and feared statement of all will be?

"Maybe it's the wiring"

True story. I've given many presentations regarding this subject and when I get to this point, right after I mention T&M and the wiring statement, I look around and notice the twitching and bulging eyes of the managers in attendance.

So, yes, ideally it's a forever loving relationship. But if not, know what timeframe you have until the divorce is finalized.

Potential Pitfall (3): The Loaner Equipment: In the event a system component fails, either by end-of-life, vandalism or any other reason, the contractor should provide a loaner component. Typically, a reputable company will supply these items at no charge if under a service agreement. However, there were cases where charges were incurred for these devices. This one question could avoid problems and save significant money if understood from the beginning.

Potential Pitfall (4): System Enhancements: During the life of the service/maintenance agreement there may be a need for upgrading protection by installing additional components. These additions will add to the cost of the agreement and modify, by extension, the expiration date.

In some cases the agreement may incur a new start date and continue for five years from the date of executing the component additions. This line item may be crucial if your organization is contemplating switching service vendors.

11. Contractor References: This portion of the RFP should address past projects the contractor successfully completed. The reference should be for a similar type of system and close dollar amount. It is of utmost importance each reference be verified prior to award. The following is an example for this section:

TYPE OF INSTALLATION/SERVICE				TOTAL DOLLAR AMOUNT

BUSINESS NAME	ADDRESS	CITY	STATE	ZIP

TELEPHONE	FACSIMILE		WEBSITE	

CONTACT PERSON	TITLE	TELEPHONE	EMAIL ADDRESS

12. Total Project Costs: This section indicates the total installed price points and payment terms for the entire project. A sample is provided below:

TOTAL PROPOSED COST

ITEM DESCRIPTION	TOTAL ASSOCIATED COST
DIGITAL IMAGING SYSTEM	$
ACCESS CONTROL SYSTEM	$

TOTAL COST FOR PROTECTION UPGRADE (DO NOT INCLUDE TAX) $_____

TOTAL COST WRITTEN-OUT _____
(EXAMPLE: ONE HUNDRED SEVENTY-NINE THOUSAND FOUR HUNDRED TEN DOLLARS AND EIGHTY-NINE CENTS)

PAYMENT TERMS

PAYMENT TYPE	TIME FRAME	PAYMENT DUE	COMMENTS
		$	
		$	
		$	
		$	

13. Contractor Submittals & Certification: The last portion of the RFP document should be the required proposal attachments and contractor certification. In addition, organizations soliciting proposals may want to have the proposal sworn before a Notary Public within their applicable jurisdiction. The following illustrates this point:

```
REQUIRED ATTACHMENTS

THE FOLLOWING DOCUMENTATION WILL NEED TO BE SUBMITTED:

1. COMPLETED AND SIGNED RESIDENTIAL PROTECTION PROPOSAL

2. COPY OF CURRENT INSURANCE CERTIFICATES

3. MANUFACTURES SPECIFICATION SHEETS AND BROCHURES FOR PROPOSED SYSTEM COMPONENTS

4. PROPRIETARY/ORGANIZATION-SPECIFIC PROPOSALS

5. SPECIFICATION ADJUSTMENT REQUEST FORM
```

```
I CERTIFY THAT I HAVE READ AND FULLY UNDERSTAND THE ENCLOSED SPECIFICATION DOCUMENT FOR THE
OUTLINED INSTALLATION SERVICES. I FURTHER CERTIFY THAT I HAVE SUBMITTED THE PROPER
DOCUMENTATION AS REQUESTED AND I AM AUTHORIZED TO ENTER INTO AN AGREEMENT AND BINDING CONTRACT
FOR THE ORGANIZATION DEFINED WITHIN THIS DOCUMENT. I UNDERSTAND THAT THIS DOCUMENT REPRESENTS
ONLY A PROPOSAL AND NOT AN AUTHORIZATION TO COMMENCE WORK.

I FURTHER UNDERSTAND AND IT IS AGREED THAT XYZ CORPORATION MAY ELECT TO MODIFY THE
SPECIFICATION AT ANYTIME AND/OR TERMINATE THE PROJECT ALTOGETHER. IT IS UNDERSTOOD AND AGREED
THAT XYZ CORPORATION IS UNDER NO OBLIGATION TO PURSUE INSTALLATION SERVICES FOR THIS
SOLICITATION.

IN ADDITION, IT IS UNDERSTOOD AND AGREED THE AWARDED CONTRACTOR WILL HAVE THE ULTIMATE
RESPONSIBILITY TO ENSURE ALL SYSTEMS ARE COMPLETELY OPERATIONAL AND IS IN COMPLIANCE WITH
ELECTRICAL AND/OR BUILDING CODE REQUIREMENTS AS WELL AS APPLICABLE LAWS.
```

```
SIGNED THIS _____ DAY OF _____ 20_____        AS AGENT FOR:_____

_____               ADDRESS:_____

SIGNATURE OF AUTHORIZED REPRESENTATIVE         _____

_____               TELEPHONE:_____

PRINT NAME AND CORPORATE TITLE
```

The Specification Adjustment Request (SAR)

As previously stated, the protection industry has grown at a rapid pace. Innovative technologies are continuing to be developed and improved on a daily basis worldwide. As a protection consultant, I have seen these changes first-hand. The numerous trade shows I have attended only confirm this upward and ever-evolving trend.

Contractors tasked with installing their respective security systems also attend industry shows. They receive preliminary orientation and training directly from manufactures representatives showcasing the latest technological advances. The Specification Adjustment Request allows a formal way to suggest changes within the Specification and RFP. This open forum ensures a system of checks and balances for the overall success of the project and ultimately end-user happiness.

The following offers an example:

CRIMINAL INTELLIGENCE ADMINISTRATION
38-11 Ditmars Boulevard ▪ Astoria, New York 11105
Telephone: 718.541.0723 ▪ Toll Free: 800.792.7181 ▪ Facsimile: 718.504.7530
Email: ceo@protect.nyc   www.protect.nyc

SPECIFICATION ADJUSTMENT REQUEST

Solicitation Identification:	RFP-00000000-R/O
Site Identification:	XYZ Corporation
Physical Location:	XXXX East Anywhere Avenue
	Anytown, State 12345

REQUEST DATE: _____

BUSINESS NAME	ADDRESS	CITY	STATE	ZIP

TELEPHONE	FACSIMILE	WEBSITE

CONTACT PERSON	TITLE	TELEPHONE	EMAIL

THE FOLLOWING SPECIFICATION ADJUSTMENTS ARE REQUESTED:

PAGE #	ADJUSTMENT REQUEST	REASON	PROPOSED ACTION

The Project Timeline

Within your Specification and Request for Proposals document there will need to be established appointments and deadlines. These dates and times are subject to revision based upon when you are ready to finalize and begin the distribution process to entities within your Bidders List. Items of concern are found below and particular segments will be discussed further within this publication.

1. Release Date: The release date should be noted within the document. This provides a verifiable means of reference and an official start date of the process.

2. Site Walkthrough: This appointment should be mandatory for all proposers on the project. Depending upon the size of the project, it is usually scheduled two weeks after the release of the Specification and RFP. This will allow sufficient time for vendors to review and analyze the received documents prior to the walkthrough.

3. Formal Questions & Answers: The deadline for vendor questions and answers should be set two weeks after the site walkthrough. This allows the contractors ample time to address concerns they have prior to submission of their respective proposals.

4. Proposal Deadline: This date should be a firm-fixed deadline and applied to all contractors without exception. Although there may be times it is appropriate to extend the deadline, all contractors should be afforded the extension. Usually, the deadline is set three weeks after the responses to the Q&A are released.

The Bidders List

Before we move further into our process, let's review what we have completed and worked on so far. We have determined our threats, met our legal and moral obligations, systematically identified our vulnerabilities, carefully crafted our budget and wrote a Specification and RFP.

We have even provided a formal means for our proposers to adjust the Specification. In addition, we have identified our appointments and deadlines which are now incorporated within our document.

It's now time to establish our Bidders List. This document must be carefully constructed and contain applicable contact information for all viable proposers on the project. But who should be on the list? How many entities should I invite to bid on the project?

The answers to these questions lye within the following:

1. Type of Project: Are you installing an access control system? Surveillance technology or intercoms? Depending upon the type of system you would like to install, you will want to contact reputable specialists within that particular area. Remember the references portion of the RFP? Those references should include demonstrated expertise within that particular protection realm.

2. Type of Location: Will the systems be installed in a residential setting? A high-rise commercial office tower? A sporting arena? Each specific venue has related specialists that cater to the facility's unique needs.

3. National Company vs. Small Business: Depending upon your comfort level and unique needs, the decision to go "national" or "small shop" when contemplating who should be invited to bid on your project will need to be resolved at this point. The following offers a brief glimpse into the issues of each of the three major types:

A. National Company: The major players. These organizations have the means and capabilities to professionally install your respective systems. The only drawback I've found, other than a sometimes inflated price, is that if the project isn't super huge, you won't get the personalized attention offered mainly to their larger customers.

B. Regional Company: These are the entities that specialize within their respective markets, have a multistate interest within the industry and may still offer the "you're important to us" feel. Most times I lean toward a regional for protection projects.

C. Small Business: Within the security industry there is a term called "trunk slammer" the traditional shop may have one employee and if you're lucky, a helper. The term was derived from a person going to their car, opening the trunk, removing a camera or two, slamming the trunk closed and off to work they go. This type of operation works best for a small project where a minimal amount of resources are needed. However, should a multifaceted and highly technical project be specified, this type of organization should absolutely be excluded. Cost overruns, scheduling conflicts and personnel issues will undoubtedly occur and project delays will most certainly happen.

4. Bidder Quantity: The size, type and complexity of the specific project determines how many organizations are invited to bid. Usually, as a matter of course, I set the list to a minimum of ten entities that are invited for an average $500,000 project. This provides a number that is easily managed and creates a vast pool of viable candidates.

The following offers a sample portion of a Bidders List entry:

CRIMINAL INTELLIGENCE ADMINISTRATION
38-11 Ditmars Boulevard ▪ Astoria, New York 11105
Telephone: 718.541.0723 ▪ Toll Free: 800.792.7181 ▪ Facsimile: 718.504.7530
Email: ceo@protect.nyc   www.protect.nyc

XYZ CORPORATION
BIDDERS LIST

Solicitation Identification:	RFP-00000000-R/O
Site Identification:	XYZ Corporation
Physical Location:	XXXX East Anywhere Avenue
	Anytown, State 12345

1. **Entity:** Any Security Entity
   Address: OOOOO Street • Any City, State 12345
   Telephone: 555.555.1212
   Facsimile: 555.555.1212
   Website: www.insertsitehere.com

Contact: John Q. Public
Cellular: 555.555.1212
Email: johnqpublic@insertsitehere.com

NOTES: _____

_____

_____

Distribution

After we have established our list of potential contractors, we are now at the point of distribution. There are several means at our disposal we may utilize for this process. The following offers a glimpse into each one:

1. Print/Mail: The process of printing, copying and eventually mailing each package provides the most cumbersome and expensive means available. In today's ecofriendly environment, this is by far not the preferred method of distribution.

2. Electronic Media: The creation of a Digital Versatile Disc (DVD) provides a viable method of "hardcopy" distribution. However, damage resulting from shipment has been known to occur and may create an issue with the aforementioned project timeline.

3. Electronic Mail: The method of distributing the package through email has been a proven technique for years. Management will also have an option to include an executive summary within the message body, complete with applicable deadline and appointment information. In addition, potential vendors can simply reply to the message confirming receipt.

4. Cloud-Based Files: The creation of an account on a file sharing network creates an easy way to share the Specification and RFP package. This cost efficient method allows large files to be shared and offers a login/password protected option.

The Walkthrough

After we have distributed the Specification/RFP packages to the respective proposers within our Bidders List, it is now time to prepare for the walkthrough. As previously stated, this should be a mandatory appointment for any and all organizations wishing to provide a proposal for the project. Imagine this appointment being optional, a contractor submitting a "blind" proposal and missing important parameters for the specified systems? Three words: delays, overruns and disaster!

The walkthrough should be well organized and follow the flow of the Specification. During the creation of the Specification, we outlined where applicable technology should be placed. We also assigned a system number for each component. The following was our example:

SUBSECTION D: Surveillance Camera Installations

I. Building Identification: XXX Boulevard

CAMERA NUMBER: I-38-001

CAMERA LOCATION: Outer Lobby Vestibule

TYPE OF INSTALLATION: New - Fixed Interior

This surveillance point shall conform to the aforementioned specifications. This dome camera will be permanently mounted to the interior ceiling. The field of view shall be the outer lobby vestibule and include images of individuals accessing the door.

The above sample of a camera installation provides a parameter for a smooth and problem-free walkthrough. Looking at just this one installation point, the contractor already knows we want a new, fixed dome camera, mounted on the interior ceiling, in the outer lobby vestibule that is watching people entering and leaving the area. We even coded the camera with "I-38-001", which means it's an "Interior-38th placed camera in the system-First within this building". This coding system will prove to be invaluable for reference and questions surrounding the system.

As a matter of course, I prepare and provide a separate Executive Overview document for all the attendees of the walkthrough. Many entities will send multiple representatives and not have given all of them full specifications for the project.

On the document, I will have a brief outline of the facility, key facts regarding the physical makeup of the property and a summary of the required components. I will also include key dates, appointments and deadlines.

After all representatives have identified themselves to me, presented business cards and signed-in on the official Roster of Attendance, I will begin my verbal presentation and welcome.

Potential Pitfall: Beware of uninvited invaders and party crashers! Yes, this has happened more times than I can count. Individuals who were not part of the Bidders List, not invited to attend the walkthrough and are seeking "a way in". On the surface it may seem harmless enough. Just a few people seeking your business. Most of them are legitimate, but I historically run projects with a competitive, closed-list and sealed bid process. There are, however, unscrupulous people with bid-rigging motivations. Yes…caught a few.

The verbal presentation will address *operational* concerns for the project. Technical questions will be deferred until the formal Question & Answer period - after the walkthrough and addressed within the next section. Decades ago, when I first started to design systems and create this process, I made the mistake of addressing all technical questions vendors had during the initial walkthrough. In one instance, this added three hours to the initial site visit. Well….live and learn! It turns out the majority of the attendees were from the sales team. Guess what? I had to repeat the answers for the engineering side of the house a week later. Yes…almost three more hours…lived and learned.

After the presentation, it's time for the physical walkthrough. This process involves walking to each and every component that will be installed within the system. Depending on security regulations and concerns for your particular environment, representatives will or will not be encouraged to photograph key installation points. As you progress through the walkthrough, pay close attention to who is actually listening to you and taking detailed notes. Usually the more interested they are in the project, they will show it by photographing and asking key operational questions.

Also, at the end of this initial site visit, see who is left. It's a sound practice to create a sign-out sheet to ensure the entire walkthrough was completed. After all, if a contractor can't be bothered with a mandatory site inspection, do you really want them on your project?

Although the official walkthrough has concluded, vendors may request another visit and inspection with their engineering team or subcontractors. Should this be allowed, a decision will need to be made on who the contact will be. Since the contractors' primary team has already inspected the site, you may want to assign a subordinate employee to show primary areas of concern. The employee will need to have full access to all locations. In addition, depending upon the scope of the project, individual contractors will most likely require an inspection of only a few locations and not the entire site.

The Formal Q&A

Throughout my years within the protection industry, I have witnessed well run projects and unfortunately, disasters. Many disastrous projects are caused by miscommunications, vague specifications and unintentional misleading scopes of work. So, now we have a well written Specification and RFP and conducted a thorough walkthrough. We have all of *OUR* ducks in a row. It's time for our contractors to align their ducks. This very critical, formal questions and answers plays a vital role in eliminating the many components for a potential nightmare. This process ensures all of the proposers are on the same page as us and provides another check and balance for our project.

Earlier within this publication we developed a timeline for our project. Specifically, we noted the following:

3. Formal Questions & Answers: The deadline for vendor questions and answers should be set two weeks after the site walkthrough. This allows the contractors ample time to address concerns they have prior to submission of their respective proposals.

So, during the walkthrough we advised our contractors that operational questions should be asked then and technical questions through a formal Q&A.

This process instructs all proposers to formally submit all questions via email and request a confirmation receipt via electronic reply. Once all questions have been received, all should be answered on letterhead and distributed via email to each and every contractor with a confirmation of receipt.

Potential Pitfall: **Many contractors will attempt to ask questions over the telephone rather than take the time for an emailed version. Although their intentions may be sincere, be very careful of your verbal commitment for a clarification or interpretation. As a matter of policy, you should direct them to send the question in writing as per the project guidelines. Beware…a simple verbal statement can be misconstrued and may come back to bite you once the project is underway**

The Proposals

We are now ready to receive the contractors proposals. Depending upon your organizations specific protocol when running RFP's, whether it's opening them upon receipt or at a formal bid opening, we must ensure the proposals integrity. It is highly recommended all proposals be stored within a locked enclosure or at least inside a locked managerial office.

Upon the opening of each proposal, a clearly defined checklist should be readily available. The checklist should include the vendors name and applicable attachments that were specified within the RFP. The below represents items we required within our previously discussed example:

REQUIRED ATTACHMENTS

THE FOLLOWING DOCUMENTATION WILL NEED TO BE SUBMITTED:

1. COMPLETED AND SIGNED RESIDENTIAL PROTECTION PROPOSAL

2. COPY OF CURRENT INSURANCE CERTIFICATES

3. MANUFACTURES SPECIFICATION SHEETS AND BROCHURES FOR PROPOSED SYSTEM COMPONENTS

4. PROPRIETARY/ORGANIZATION-SPECIFIC PROPOSALS

5. SPECIFICATION ADJUSTMENT REQUEST FORM

Once all proposals are opened and "checked-in" we are ready for the analysis.

The Analysis

First, let's take a closer look at our required attachments and why each one is important:

1. Completed and Signed Residential Protection Proposal: This document is yours. It represents all the information that is important for this phase, the analysis. In one complete, compact form you will know vital information regarding your potential contractor. In addition, this form streamlines the analysis because all the requested information is systematically located in the exact same place as all the other proposals.

2. Copy of Current Insurance Certificates: Receiving an official CoI at the proposal phase ensures the contractor has current insurance meeting your organizations' requirements. There is no need, at this phase, to have the certificate issued in your company name or contain any noted additionally insured parties.

3. Manufactures Specification Sheets and Brochures for Proposed System Components: These "cut sheets" are absolutely vital and contain a wealth of information. Contractors should be required to provide a sheet for each and every component they are installing. The documents encompass power requirements, features and dimensions. Dimensions? Yes, remember the HUGE, UGLY and GINORMOUS camera example. Here's our first clue.

4. Proprietary/Organization-Specific Proposals: By reviewing these documents we gain insight into the contractor's organizational and business skills. We can evaluate corporate structure, consistency and even literacy and compare them to the standards of the other bidders. This will give us a well-rounded analysis and provide an element for award.

5. Specification Adjustment Request Form: This form is part of the entire RFP package and should be returned either filled-out or initialed with no proposed changes. This provides consistency, ensures changes were not overlooked and maintains integrity of the process.

Just a little heads-up on what you may encounter during this analysis. As previously mentioned, I usually send out packages to at least ten interested and qualified contractors. Why the magic number ten? Historically, I've found the following happens:

A. Two contractors who said they were "very" interested, now withdrew and vanished.

B. One proposal is from a contractor who thought the installation was on Mars and adjusted their pricing for space travel.

C. One contractors' proposal was so low they would probably hemorrhage money and either cut corners or totally walk-off the job.

D. One proposal didn't contain any attachments and will be marked "unresponsive".

E. The final five. These proposals may have very similar pricing and component quality.

As previously stated, the first parts of the proposal I turn to are the "total installed price" and cost for the annual service agreements. This not only determines if the contractor is attempting to "buy the job" but also ensures budgetary considerations are met. Also, these sections give me a sense of where the project is headed based upon the cost analysis. The next portion of the document I turn to will be the Certificate of Insurance and, if required, the bonding level of the company. This preliminary perusal lets me know if the contractor will be "in the running" for the project.

After the preliminaries, it's time for the actual analysis. This process involves ensuring each question is answered throughout the RFP document.

Potential Pitfall: **Absolutely beware of the "to be determined" or similar responses to questions. This "answer" may wreak havoc when it comes to contract award or in the worst case…after the project has started.**

Remember, you have carefully created a Specification and Request for Proposals document. Everything surrounding the project has been addressed. These types of responses signify either the contractor doesn't know the answer, never bothered to research their response or maybe seeking a change order once the project has commenced. Imagine the "TBD" responses to questions such as number of work crews, completion time frame, or any combination of the installation costs. Yes. Potential disaster.

Once you've analyzed the proposals and marked off key questions you have for the contractors, it's time for the spreadsheet. The document headers may be adjusted depending upon your individual preferences and what your organization considers key elements for award. The following example illustrates spreadsheet captions:

OVERVIEW 1

COMPANY IDENTIFICATION	STATE/YEAR OF INCORPORATION	BANKRUPTCY/ CONVICTION?	P/EMPLOYMENT INVESTIGATIONS?	DRUG/ALCOHOL POLICY?	BONDED EMPLOYEES?	INSURANCE REQUIREMENTS MET?	SUBCONTRACTORS PROPOSED?

OVERVIEW 2

COMPANY IDENTIFICATION	NUMBER OF CREWS/PERSONS	NUMBER OF SUPERVISORS	PROPOSED LABOR	AUTHORIZED REPRESENTATIVE?	TRAINING COMPLETED?	REQUIRED LEAD TIME FRAME	COMPLETION TIME FRAME

OVERVIEW 3

COMPANY IDENTIFICATION	SPECIFICATION COMPLIANT?	SPECIFICATION ADJUSTMENT SUBMITTED?	PROJECT MANAGER INDICATED?	MANUFACTURES WARRANTEE	TOTAL INSTALLED COST	ANNUAL SERVICE AGREEMENT	LOANER EQUIPMENT?/ CHARGE?

MISCELLANEOUS PROPOSAL PARAMETERS

COMPANY IDENTIFICATION	RESPONSE TIME NORMAL/AFTER-HOURS/EMERGENCY	EMERGENCY CALLS - COST (PER HOUR)	PERFORMANCE BONDING /COST	ARCHITECTURAL DRAWINGS? TOTAL COST	ADDITIONAL COPIES (FIVE) COST	REFERENCES PROVIDED?	ALL REQUIRED DOCUMENTATION SUBMITTED?

The Vendor Selection Conference

We have now completed "the grunt work". The Specification, RFP, walkthrough, formal Q&A and proposal analysis will provide for a solid contract award and thus, a "well-oiled" project.

It is now time for the Vendor Selection Conference. At this point, most of our questions and concerns have been answered and addressed within the preceding documents. This conference will provide a forum for the contractors to demonstrate their particular systems, give a presentation to your Board of Directors or senior management and afford clarification on residual issues.

The selection conference should be geared toward the contractors' presentation first and a question and answer period thereafter. The Q&A is a virtual interview and should be initiated by the Board, senior management or perhaps invited committee members.

Depending upon the size and complexity of the project, I usually allow for a thirty minute presentation, thirty minute Q&A and thirty minutes of discussion after the contractor has left the room. This will allow sufficient time to address concerns and prevent contractor overlaps.

Potential Pitfall 1: Contractors employ professional sales people whose sole purpose is to sell the customer. Sometimes, unfortunately, by any means necessary. It's just what they do.

I was running a rather complex and high-end RFP for an installation of a surveillance system within a commercial building. It was time for the conference and, oh-boy was the sales team for this one particular contractor ready! Seven, yes seven, sales people stood tall in their expensive suits, had a team of operational employees assemble their system for a full demonstration and handed out additional literature on their firm. Undoubtedly, a very impressive "show of force".

The presentation went off without a hitch and all in attendance were wide-eyed and excited with the system. As a matter of fact, everyone LOVED the system! Not to mention the amazingly articulate sales force in the room. I would bet dollars-to-donuts that if a contract were ready to be signed it absolutely would have been on-the-spot!

So….I had to ask the question that I pretty much knew the answer to already.

"The system that you demonstrated, is that the one you are proposing to install"?

The room went silent. My clients' eyes shifted from me back to the sales team. Then, one member of the team answered, after what seemed like an eternity. Well…no…but it's similar.

Yes…another question.

"Will the system you are proposing to install have all of the features you just demonstrated"?

The answer was simple and infuriating. No, it won't…you will have to upgrade.

Upgrade? BEFORE the award? The contractor went from the favorite child to automatic disqualification. With just two questions.

Interview parameters during the question and answer period should address concerns and the dreaded "to be determined" answers within the RFP document. Additional questions which may be asked include those which may reveal hidden fees, potential pitfalls and headaches after the initial installation. Some of these include:

1. Accounts vs. Service Trucks. During the process a contractor may reveal, or be asked directly, what is the total number of active accounts they currently service. Usually, contractors are inclined to boast about the many active customers they have. A follow-up question to their response is absolutely paramount. "How may service trucks do you have"?

Should the contractor, for example, state they have 300 active service contracts but only 3 trucks, you will most likely experience long delays for service. A good ratio of 10% service trucks vs. active accounts will be sufficient to achieve a good service response.

2. Software. Notice how this word rhymes with…..nightmare. Should this item not be properly addressed, that's exactly what you will live through. This is an absolute. Technology on the market today, cameras, monitors, recorders burglar alarms and access control systems all rely on software to operate. This specialized software, just like any computer, requires updates and upgrades as time wears on. Three of the more common pitfalls regarding this necessity includes:

A. Annual Licensing & Charges. Depending on the manufacturer, system and installing company, there may be an annual charge for firmware upgrades. This charge should be well understood, accepted as an additional line item or be included within the service agreement. However it is agreed upon it will need to be well documented within the subsequent contracts.

Imagine missing this one parameter and a year after the installation you will need to pay an additional $10,000 just to have your system running. Better yet…you bought a "proprietary system" as previously discussed and now the only vendor in the country wants $35,000 per year!

B. Software Support. This potentially nasty parameter includes the support of older versions of the installed software. It should be absolutely understood if the manufacturer supports "legacy" systems for a predetermined amount of time. Just think if you bought a system and within two years, the system is considered "obsolete" and in need of replacement. Better yet, imagine buying Windows Vista or Windows XP two weeks before Microsoft shut down all support. Yes, potential nightmare.

C. Software Versions. Throughout the entire software industry, terms such as "Professional Edition", "Corporate Edition" and my all-time favorite… "Lite Edition" surface at every turn. Software versions differ greatly in features and undoubtedly in price.

Be absolutely wary of these terms. It must be clearly understood which version of software is needed to accomplish your individual goals. As a matter of course, a "Lite Edition" should never be employed within a security environment. These versions offer a minimal amount of features and may require a fee to upgrade after "the introductory offer" has expired.

3. Training. Each protection system carries their own unique training requirements. The contractor, who we _now_ know is a fully trained and "authorized manufacturer representative", should offer a training course to applicable staff members. Training costs will vary depending upon the complexity of the system, the amount of time required for training and the amount of staff to be trained. Simple systems with a handful of trainees is typically provided at no charge. Training parameters, charges and circumstances surrounding re-training should all be discussed and included within the contract.

Yes, the selection conference will enable you to see the components first hand, provide a tabletop demonstration and resolve key issues surrounding the contract award. Two other important facets of the conference…it enables you to see first-hand the contractors organizational skills and workability within your property. Having this positive synergy will provide a pathway to a happy and healthy relationship throughout the years.

The Best and Final Offer (BAFO)

Upon the successful conclusion of the conference, we are now at the point of asking our finalists for their "best and final offer". Residual questions have been answered and everyone is on the same page. This portion of our process allows the contractors to "sharpen their pencils" on their price points and may even include throwing in a few extra services for free. Yes, competition at its best.

The BAFO document should be a simple one page form allowing for easy analysis and ultimately contract award. It is important to note, during this phase the price for all elements should _decrease_.

However, if items were overlooked during the Specification and RFP phase and clarified during the conference, it is possible this will provide an *increase* in costs. This is usually due to a misunderstanding of the project requirements by not more than one contractor.

The following offers a sample of a Best and Final Offer document:

CRIMINAL INTELLIGENCE ADMINISTRATION
38-11 Ditmars Boulevard ▪ Astoria, New York 11105
Telephone: 718.541.0723 ▪ Toll Free: 800.792.7181 ▪ Facsimile: 718.504.7530
Email: ceo@protect.nyc   www.protect.nyc

BEST AND FINAL OFFER

Solicitation Identification:	RFP-00000000-R/O
Site Identification:	XYZ Corporation
Physical Location:	XXXX East Anywhere Avenue
	Anytown, State 12345

ENTITY IDENTIFICATION: _____

I CERTIFY THAT I HAVE READ AND FULLY UNDERSTAND THE SPECIFICATION DOCUMENTS FOR THE ABOVE REFERENCED SOLICITATIONS. I FURTHER CERTIFY THAT I HAVE SUBMITTED THE PROPER DOCUMENTATION AS REQUESTED AND I AM AUTHORIZED TO ENTER INTO AN AGREEMENT AND BINDING CONTRACT FOR THE ORGANIZATION DEFINED WITHIN THIS DOCUMENT. I UNDERSTAND THAT THIS DOCUMENT REPRESENTS ONLY A PROPOSAL AND NOT AN AUTHORIZATION TO COMMENCE WORK.

IN ADDITION, IT IS UNDERSTOOD AND AGREED THE AWARDED CONTRACTOR WILL HAVE THE ULTIMATE RESPONSIBILITY TO ENSURE ALL SYSTEMS ARE COMPLETELY OPERATIONAL AND IS IN COMPLIANCE WITH ELECTRICAL AND/OR BUILDING CODE REQUIREMENTS AS WELL AS APPLICABLE LAWS.

DIGITAL IMAGING SYSTEM:

    A. TOTAL INSTALLED COST: $ _____

    B. PERFORMANCE & PAYMENT BOND COSTS: $ _____

--------------TOTAL COST: $ _____

   C. ANNUAL MAINTENANCE/SERVICE AGREEMENT COST: $ _____

TOTAL INSTALLED PROJECT (INCLUDING BONDS) COST: $ _____

TOTAL COST WRITTEN-OUT _____
(EXAMPLE: ONE HUNDRED SEVENTY-NINE THOUSAND FOUR HUNDRED TEN DOLLARS AND EIGHTY-NINE CENTS)

I FURTHER CERTIFY THE ABOVE PRICING SCHEDULE REFLECTS A TRUE AND ACCURATE ACCOUNT FOR THE COMPLETE INSTALLATION OF THE ENTIRE DIGITAL IMAGING SYSTEM. IN ADDITION, IT IS AGREED THE NOTED SERVICE AGREEMENT WILL BE IMPLEMENTED AND CHARGED UPON THE SECOND YEAR FOLLOWING INSTALLATION. THE FIRST TWELVE (12) MONTHS AFTER INSTALLATION WILL NOT INCUR ANY CHARGE FOR REPLACEMENT AND/OR REPAIR OF DEFECTIVE/FAILED SYSTEM COMPONENTS.

```
SIGNED THIS _____ DAY OF _____ 20_____        AS AGENT FOR:_____

_____      ADDRESS:_____

SIGNATURE OF AUTHORIZED REPRESENTATIVE         _____

_____      TELEPHONE:_____

PRINT NAME AND CORPORATE TITLE
```

The BAFO Analysis

The analysis of the Best and Final Offer submittals should include a formalized document which clearly shows each contractors price points and relative ranking. The document should not only rank initial installation costs but should also show a *total* cost, with applicable service/maintenance agreements, for the *"five-year plan"*. Remember, at this stage the contractor may *lower* their initial installation price and *raise* the service agreement cost. The five-year plan will prevent the aforementioned "buying of the job".

The following is an example if the BAFO analysis document:

CRIMINAL INTELLIGENCE ADMINISTRATION
38-11 Ditmars Boulevard ▪ Astoria, New York 11105
Telephone: 718.541.0723 ▪ Toll Free: 800.792.7181 ▪ Facsimile: 718.504.7530
Email: ceo@protect.nyc   www.protect.nyc

BAFO ANALYSIS

Solicitation Identification: **RFP-00000000-R/O**
Site Identification: **XYZ Corporation**
Physical Location: **XXXX East Anywhere Avenue**
    Anytown, State 12345

The following represents an analysis of the Best and Final Offer documents received by the invited organizations:

A. Cost Ranking (Primary BAFO's):

RANKING	ENTITY IDENTIFICATION	INSTALLATION COST	SERVICE AGREEMENT	TOTAL FIVE YEAR COST
1	XXXXXXXXXX	$455,163.	$30,000	$605,163.
2	YYYYYYYYYY	$460,878.25	$41,280.	$667,278.25
3	*ZZZZZZZZZZ*	$482,264.06	$27,389.77	$619,212.91

B. Five Year Cost BAFO Ranking:

XXXXXXXXXX
ZZZZZZZZZZ
YYYYYYYYYY

The Best and Final Offer is the last document the contractor will submit prior to contract award. It is extremely important to ensure the design of the system is adequate, any pitfalls have been addressed, you are very satisfied with the proposed technology and comfortable with the installation company and subcontractors. Should any of these components be questionable….STOP!

This phase of the project still allows you to make changes. At this point you may want to eliminate a few cameras, add access control readers or relocate several key burglar components. Should you wish to modify the current scope of the project, all you will need to do is incorporate an Addendum into the existing Specification. The Addendum can be from a few minor changes to the incorporation of an entirely new add-on system. This will be your last chance before contract. By moving forward with the project you will begin to incur legal expenses for contracts, pay applicable project deposits and any changes after this point may require *dreaded change orders*.

The following offers a sample Addendum:

CRIMINAL INTELLIGENCE ADMINISTRATION
38-11 Ditmars Boulevard ▪ Astoria, New York 11105
Telephone: 718.541.0723 ▪ Toll Free: 800.792.7181 ▪ Facsimile: 718.504.7530
Email: ceo@protect.nyc   www.protect.nyc

SOLICITATION ADDENDUM
JANUARY 28, 2016

Solicitation Identification: RFP-00000000-R/O

Site Identification: XYZ Corporation

Physical Location: XXXX East Anywhere Avenue

Anytown, State 12345

I. Digital Imaging System - Subsection E (Surveillance Camera Installations)

A. The following represents an <u>additional</u> interior camera installation:

Building Identification: XXXX East Anywhere Avenue

      CAMERA NUMBER: A-I-011 (A)

      CAMERA LOCATION: Interior Hallway @ Garage Door

      TYPE OF INSTALLATION: New – Fixed – Ceiling Mount

      This surveillance point shall conform to the original specifications. This fixed dome camera will be permanently mounted to the interior ceiling. The field of view shall include persons accessing the garage door.

  B. The following represents a <u>modified</u> interior camera installation:

Building Identification: XXXX East Anywhere Avenue

      CAMERA NUMBER: A-I-029

      CAMERA LOCATION: Inner Hallway @ Staircase "C"

      TYPE OF INSTALLATION: New – PTZ – Ceiling Mount

      This surveillance point shall conform to the original specifications. This PTZ camera will be permanently mounted to the interior ceiling. The field of view shall include persons accessing the interior hallway.

Once you have issued an Addendum to the project, it will be necessary to reissue the Best and Final Offer document and repeat the analysis accordingly.

The Change Order

Before continuing onto the contract portion, I would like to cover project Change Orders. These orders, formally, as the name implies, change components of the project. These changes may involve adding technology, relocating system components or resolving an "unforeseen circumstance". Wait, an unforeseen circumstance?

I am of the strict belief that if a contractor submits a bid and agrees to a price point, they assume responsibility for the successful project. Remember when we had the contractors submit *OUR* RFP form? There is one statement on that form and reiterated on the BAFO document which safeguards us against the "unforeseen circumstances". That signed and certified statement is simply *"IT IS UNDERSTOOD AND AGREED THE AWARDED CONTRACTOR WILL HAVE THE ULTIMATE RESPONSIBILITY TO ENSURE ALL SYSTEMS ARE COMPLETELY OPERATIONAL"*.

Now, having said that, there may come a time in the project where _you_ will want changes. Let's say, for example, you want additional interior cameras. Included within the original Specification, we asked for an uninstalled unit cost and an hourly billable rate for services as follows:

MANUFACTURER	MODEL NUMBER	DESCRIPTION	UNINSTALLED UNIT COST

ITEM DESCRIPTION	TOTAL HOURLY COST
TECHNICAL ASSISTANCE (SOFTWARE)	$
GENERAL HOURLY BILL RATE FOR SERVICES	$

We now have a general idea of how much the additions will cost. It is important to note, whenever a Change Order is authorized it should be in writing. As a matter of choice, I prefer to write an official Addendum, include agreed upon pricing and incorporate a signed version within the original Specification. This way everything is understood and wrapped up nice and tidy.

The Contract

We have finally reached the part of a legally binding contract. This is the final stage of the process and involves officially awarding the project to the successful contractor. It is _HIGHLY_ recommended that corporate counsel draw up this document. Contractors have their own versions of contracts that are generically prepared. Unless you are installing just two or three cameras, these types of contracts should _NEVER_ be signed. They spell out practically every protection for the contractor and absolutely none for you. Please remember, the contract is the lifeblood of the project and should issues arise, will ultimately determine either a positive or negative outcome.

The contract should be clearly written and encompass the parameters for the entire project. The original Specification, RFP form, issued Addendums and BAFO documents should be included as separate attachments and referenced within the contract.

In addition, any modifications or clarifications of the original documents should be clearly spelled out within the contractual document. Although this publication does not seek to offer legal advice and should never be construed as an alternative to counsel, the following represents an outline of what should be included:

1. Contractual Parties: This portion of the document spells out the "Who" of the contract. This section includes the date of the contract, organizational names, addresses and applicable contact information.

2. Scope of Work: This segment comprises of an overview of all work to be preformed. The "What" aspect involves a synopsis of the Specification and references all attachments.

3. Location of Project: The "Where" section clearly defines all physical addresses and work locations. Should the project encompass multiple locations, each address should be listed separately.

4. Work Scheduling and Time-Frame: From start date to total completion. This portion clearly defines applicable time frames. The "When" segment also indicates the days of week the contractor is authorized to work and includes "normal working hours" clauses.

Potential Pitfall: Here we go…a rather medium-sized project was being completed by a nationally recognized security contractor. The installation involved multiple surveillance devices and was running quite smoothly. As the project seemed like it was nearly complete, the technicians became scarce and the managing agent was becoming increasingly anxious. I received a call and was asked to review the project and to provide guidance. Upon reviewing the contract, the very well prepared contract, I noticed one very important item was missing. The contract clearly defined the start and completion dates and had all the legalese you could stand. What it didn't have was a penalty clause should the installation fail to be completed within that time-frame.

There was absolutely nothing, short of refusing to pay the agreed upon amounts and starting a legal battle, the managing agent was able to do. Well, my intervention did help to speed the project to completion and everything was eventually worked out. But, what if it didn't?

A clearly defined penalty clause should always be written into the contract. I usually recommend liquidated damages of $100-$250 per day, depending on the complexity of the project. This clause absolutely motivates the contractor to finish the installation within the agreed upon time-frame.

5. Project-Specific Problematic Areas: Sometimes protection technology is utilized and installed within a specific problematic area for an explicit expected result. I've seen this especially within residential housing communities. Usually, it involves perpetrators committing criminal acts within specific areas of the property. This section, "Why", is utilized to address expected outcomes of the employed technology. Please note, installing companies are not insurance agencies and cannot, under any circumstances, guarantee a crime-free area. This section merely addresses the anticipated outcome.

6. The Installation Plan: This portion of the contract spells out, either by written word or attached architectural drawings, the "How" of the project. It involves a detailed installation plan and encompasses all that is required for the complete installation and completion of the project.

7. Contract Price and Payments: The total contractual price and applicable progressive payments are indicated in detail within this section. Please note, all values should be numerical and written out in word form to ensure accuracy. As a matter of course, I usually authorize quarterly payments as per the following schedule:

A. Mobilization and Deposit: Due upon the successful execution of the contract.

B. Delivery and Storage of Technology: Paid within thirty days after delivery, inspection and acceptance of all system components.

C. Progressive Payment: Approved when greater than sixty percent of the total completion of the project has been inspected.

D. Final Payment: Ratified when the total project has been completed, inspected and each component tested.

8. Service Agreement/Maintenance Clause: The parameters for the maintenance and service agreement should be clearly defined and incorporated within the contract. It is important to indicate price-points for the annual agreement and include the applicable monthly/semiannual payment schedule. Also included within this section, are the effective dates, mandatory response times, applicable loaner equipment charges and a *CANCELATION* clause. This clause is paramount in case the contractor doesn't live up to the agreement.

9. Insurance Requirements: Depending upon your organizations specific requirements, parameters for general liability, worker's compensation and automobile liability insurance should be included within a separate clause of the contract. Specifically, mandatory minimum amounts should be indicated and guarantees of renewals upon expiration. In addition, should performance and/or payment bonds be required, it is imperative they are included within the contract.

All applicable Certificates of Insurance (with additional insured) and Bonds should be provided no later than two weeks after the contract execution.

10. Labor Relations: The inclusion of a clause directing the contractor to assume any and all liability surrounding their employed or subcontracted labor cannot be overemphasized. Project delays involving job actions, labor contract disputes and wage issues should be the sole responsibility of the awarded contractor.

The aforementioned parameters offer a glimpse into the well prepared contractual document.

Additional items corporate attorneys may include within the contract are indemnification clauses, termination of project parameters, storage of equipment, as well as a host of legal liability passages. It is strongly advised and should be a standard practice to consult an attorney for the preparation of any contracts.

Once the contract is prepared and submitted to the contractor for review, it's time for their legal representative to review the document and offer their viewpoint. Typically, the "legalese" portions will be negotiated between the respective legal teams. Usually, items of concern involve the wording of clauses centering on liability and indemnification. Once all the negotiations are complete and a final contract is prepared, it's finally time to sign on the "dotted line".

The contract signing may either be a formalized meeting where all parties sign their respective copies or as simple as an emailed document instructing the contractor to prepare the required copies, execute them and return them for co-signature. Once received and co-executed, we are ready to start the project!

The Project Commencement

Eureka!!! We have finally signed our contract and officially awarded the job to the most qualified contractor with the most cost-efficient price point! All the hard work we have put in so far…finally…will pay off.

The project commencement, just like all other steps we've taken, involves a systematic approach. Typically, the appointed Project Manager will have a preliminary meeting with the contractor. This occurs before the formal kickoff meeting, which actually *officially* starts the project. The preliminary meeting is usually conducted onsite and involves the necessary documentation which was indicated during the RFP process.

This documentation will need to be presented prior to the kickoff meeting. These documents include:

1. Mobilization and Deposit Invoice: The first authorized invoice for the project should be presented after the contract is signed and well before the kickoff meeting. It is recommended that a form be created detailing particulars, such as date, project number, invoice number and reason for payment, to ensure sound recordkeeping. The American Institute of Architects have created many outstanding contractual documents, including their Application and Certificate for Payment, which can be downloaded from their website (aia.org) for a nominal fee.

The timely submittal and payment of the first invoice will ensure the contractor will be able to order project components and there will be no preliminary delays.

2. Certificates of Insurance: The official CoI's for the project should be presented at this point. Depending upon your organizations specific requirements, parameters for general liability, worker's compensation and automobile liability insurance should be adequately contained within the documents. The Certificate should be of standard industry format and contain applicable effective/expiration dates, additional insured parties and coverage dollar values. In addition, should subcontractors be utilized, it is imperative for them to present valid CoI's for their portion of the project.

Once all of the documents are received, a verification check should be conducted in order to validate coverage.

3. Performance and/or Payment Bonds: Earlier within this publication we mentioned that performance bonds ensure the awarded contractor completes the installation professionally and within the scope of work. In addition, we also indicated that in order to ensure subcontractors are paid properly, we may require the issuance of a payment bond.

Upon the signing of the contract, the contractor should have initiated the bond process should one or both be required. The issued documents should also be verified upon receipt.

After the preliminary meeting with the contractor, a full comprehensive walkthrough should be performed. The walkthrough should start at the beginning of the Specification and follow an unobstructed course. Each point within the system should be thoroughly examined and any potential issues addressed.

Upon the successful conclusion of the walkthrough and the submittal of all required documents, the Project Manager should meet with managerial representatives of the property. This preliminary meeting helps ensure a seamless kickoff and streamlines the official start of the project. Copies of the aforementioned verified documents should be readily available and originals kept within a secured project file along with the originals of the RFP, proposals and contract.

The following items should be discussed and an action plan initiated:

1. Document Review: The initial invoice, insurance certificates and bonds should be discussed and approved.

2. Available Parking Facilities: The availability of parking for the employees of the contractor and applicable work trucks should be discussed. Ideally, parking should be reserved and located within close proximity of applicable project locations.

3. Storage Locations: Generally speaking, contractors prefer to store system components, tools, wire and hardware onsite. Optimally, a dedicated and locked private storage room would provide the contractor with a secured location. It should be absolutely understood and included within the contract, the utilization of the provided room is at the contractors' sole risk. Property management may allow the contractor to change locking hardware to ensure they alone have access.

4. Onsite Skilled Trades: Depending upon your unique circumstances, the project may involve coordinating with other skilled trades such as electricians, carpenters and plumbers working within close proximity of the protection points. This holds absolutely true for a new-construction venture. In addition, as previously mentioned, should your facilities have elevators, then representatives from the elevator company will need to be on the project team. At a very minimum, contact information should be readily available for the Project Manager.

5. Ease of Access: Contractors working within the facility may need to access locked rooms, storage areas and/or leased tenant space. Ideally, a dedicated proprietary employee who has total access to the property should be assigned for the duration of the project. Should this not be feasible, the issuance of contractor keys should be considered in order to streamline installation and expeditiously complete the project.

6. Known Hazardous or Unsanitary Conditions: The presence of rodents, mold, insect infestation or any other known hazardous or unsanitary condition should be remedied prior to the arrival of the contractors' crew. As a matter of course, contractual employees have refused to enter locations where such conditions exist. In addition, these circumstances prove to be challenging for the maintenance of protection technology. Historically, rodents have been known to routinely chew through wiring and insect infestations may cause failure within system components.

7. Project Team: The makeup of this team will ensure success or, if not properly assembled, may lead to delays and even project failure. Generally, I like to keep the team as small as possible. The smaller the team, the more manageable the operation.

The operational core of the team should consist of the following individuals:

A. Management: A senior-level representative of the facility should spearhead the team. This individual will need to be a decision-maker for the organization. This will ensure streamlined efficiency and immediate resolution of potential problems.

70

B. Project Manager: The PM is responsible for the entire project and day-to-day supervision of the work crews. The primary job of this individual will be to ensure the components are properly installed and the crews are following the requirements of the Specification. In addition, the PM should be the primary point of contact for all phases of the project and act as the onsite facility representative throughout the venture.

C. Maintenance/Engineering: The senior representative from the proprietary maintenance/engineering staff should be included within the operational core of the team. This individual has vital and key insights regarding the inner workings of the property.

D. Contractor: A senior representative from the _operational/installation_ side of the house will need to be included on the project team. Usually, up until this point the contractors' _sales force_ has been involved. This individual is absolutely vital to ensure the technical aspects of the project are addressed in a timely fashion.

E. Skilled Trades: Representatives from other trades, such as electricians, plumbers, carpenters and elevator mechanics may be included as needed. Sometimes, as in new construction or major remodeling operations, protection companies will work in tandem with other skilled labor.

Potential Pitfall: Historically, union and non-union companies do not play well together. Careful consideration should be given when utilizing non-union labor within a new construction setting with all other trades having applicable union membership. There have been numerous accounts of wires being cut, components being damaged and other forms of vandalism which may lead to headaches and ultimately project delays.

The Project Kickoff Meeting

We have now arrived at setting a date for the official start of the project. The kickoff meeting is usually held onsite with all representatives from the aforementioned team.

At this point, all required documents have been submitted, reviewed and analyzed, potential issues addressed and we are now ready for a streamlined and organized meeting.

The Project Manager is usually tasked with scheduling the time and location, setting objectives, providing the official sign-in sheet, running the meeting and keeping the minutes.

Historically, I would arrange seating starting with senior property management to my left and assign seats clockwise in descending order of job titles and responsibilities. This systematic seating plan ensures everyone recognizes the key-players assigned to the project.

The agenda should be straightforward and encompass the following items:

A. Welcome: A brief welcome statement should be prepared for the start of the meeting. This includes an overview of the property or facility with key operational facts about the location.

B. Introductions: The introductions of the team may be made by the Project Manager or by the individuals themselves. In either case, senior management should be introduced first.

C. Project Review: An overview of the entire project will need to be conducted at this point. It will be helpful to have handouts describing the overall project parameters and expectations.

D. Project Milestones: A schedule of milestones for the project should be outlined and available for the meeting. I find it helpful to create a spreadsheet delineating applicable tasks with anticipated completion dates.

E. Communications: A clear notification and reporting system is paramount to a well-organized project. As previously stated, the PM should be the primary point of contact for all phases of the project and act as the onsite facility representative throughout the venture. This will ensure a streamlined line of communication and prevent errors and omissions throughout the project.

F. Parking Facilities: The contractor's personnel will need to be advised of the preapproved parking locations for their employees and applicable work trucks.

G. Storage Locations: Applicable preapproved storage locations for the contractor's system components, tools, wire and hardware will need to be discussed and finalized during the meeting. It should be reiterated and understood that the utilization of the provided locations are at the contractor's sole risk.

H. Access to Facility/Building Locked Areas: At this point in the meeting, the contractor should be issued the building/facility keys or be introduced to the dedicated employee who will provide direct access to locked rooms, storage areas and/or leased tenant space.

I. Project Delays: This portion of the meeting should address foreseeable risks which may cause minor suspensions of the project. Items of concern include but are not limited to the following:

1. Severe Weather Conditions: Depending upon the season or the project's particular geographic location, the threat of snow storms, torrential downpours of rain or any other severe weather will inevitably delay completion.

2. Property Labor Disputes: Active labor contracts with the property's proprietary employees which may cause job actions, strikes and/or boycott issues should be addressed. These work stoppages will cause absolute delays should the contractor's employees refuse to cross established picket lines. In addition, there may be an increased likelihood of intentional damage of installed system components committed by disgruntled employees. Security precautions should be taken to circumvent these potential events.

3. Shipping/Receiving of Components: The contractor should initiate the ordering of system components immediately upon payment of the initial invoice. This will ensure the timely delivery of all necessary components of the protection apparatus.

J. Operational Impact: This agenda item concerns minimizing the impact on normal property operations which may occur throughout the installation. The project may involve noisy core drilling or running necessary wire through leased commercial space. Portions of the installation which may disrupt normal business operations should be carefully addressed in order to minimalize potential inconvenience.

K. Questions & Answers: Upon the conclusion of agenda items for the kickoff meeting, a formal Q&A should be conducted. This will ensure the entire team is on the same page and will undoubtedly streamline the installation and ensure project success.

Potential Pitfall: One day, a large residential housing development was having a project kickoff meeting. Although I wasn't part of the project, the General Manager of this development asked me to sit-in on the meeting and offer any advice I may have.

The meeting involved replacing the exterior lobby doors and windows throughout the complex. As the well-organized meeting progressed, the portion involving an access control system was mentioned. The General Contractor briefly stated, "Oh our subcontractor for the keyfob system is here". A one line response was heard from the subcontractor "yes, but I will be last, after the doors are installed". Well, my ears perked and I looked directly at the manager, with what had to be a wide, deer-in-the-headlights look. He stopped the meeting and asked what was on my mind.

I asked and wanted to confirm if the new doors will have the same mechanical locks as the originals. The GC gave me a smug smirk, shook his head and said "no, we are installing a brand new system". I smiled and politely asked one question. "When the new doors are installed how will anyone get into the building since your subcontractor will go last"? Yes...silence fell. I went on to say that the access control subcontractor needs to be first...not last.

What needs to be accomplished immediately following the meeting will be purchasing and installing the new access control computer, creating a database for the residents and then distributing the keyfobs. Only after distribution, can the doors be installed.

Talk about project delays.

Project Management

We have now officially started the project and on our way to a successful installation. During the project management phase, the PM is responsible for ensuring the contractor has engaged the required team, is sticking to the Specification and is being paid as agreed within the contract. In addition, the PM is the primary point of contact for the project and acts as the onsite facility representative during the installation.

Throughout the project, there should be regularly scheduled progress meetings. These meetings should be held at least twice a month with *all* team members being present. Each meeting should have an official sign-in sheet and the PM should keep a record of each item discussed and create minutes for each meeting.

The meetings should address project milestones of the installation which have been completed. It is important to note, should the contractor fall behind in the beginning of the installation and miss important deadlines and milestones, they should be prepared to provide a legitimate reason for the failure. Should the contractor provide an inadequate response, they should be reminded of the contractual penalty clause as mentioned earlier within this publication.

The Project's Final Phases:

As the project progresses and draws closer to completion, the PM will need to accomplish a few tasks. These tasks, outlined below, ensure a seamless and trouble-free transition to signoff.

1. Preliminary Inspection: Upon the contractor advising of the imminent completion of the project, a _preliminary_ inspection of the entire installation should be performed by the Project Manager. The PM should visit each protection point and inspect the elements of the installation. Notes should be taken to include problematic issues and recommended corrective action.

2. The Punch List: Upon the completion of the preliminary inspection, an official "punch list" should be generated. The punch list should include all issues identified during the inspection so the contractor can take immediate action and avoid unnecessary delays.

3. Final System Test: Once all of the punch list items have been addressed and the installation has been deemed "complete" by the contractor, it's now time for the final walkthrough and testing of each and every component of the system.

Potential Pitfall: OK, stop. Just for a minute at this point. Know right from jump street that contractors want to wrap-up projects quickly and as painless as possible. I mentioned that _each and every component_ should be inspected and tested. When I am advised that a project is complete and start to perform a final inspection and test for the system, I absolutely expect all components will be functioning as intended. There should be no surprises.

During my earlier years of consulting and running projects, there is one in particular that stands out in my mind. Picture New York City, mid-August, hazy, hot and humid and well into the 90's. One particular contractor advised on the completion of a large project I was running. This project included an integrated access control, surveillance and burglar alarm system for a sprawling residential housing complex. All components of the system, within this non-air-conditioned complex, needed to work in unison to adequately secure project signoff. Well, here we go and lets start the final tests.

The beginning of the inspection and testing went quite well. Every component, located on the exterior and roofs of the buildings, which seemed like three feet from the sun, were installed properly and passed the tests with flying colors. Approaching the mid-way mark, about _three hours_ into the process, I came upon a device which wasn't operational. I looked at the contractor and they immediately sent the technician, which was accompanying us, to fix the problem. We continued to another adjoining device and…..yes…..it wasn't working either. By the way, did I mention it was mid-August, hazy, hot and humid and well into the 90's?!? The technician returned and was unable to immediately fix the problem. Here _endith_ the inspection.

The morale of my unfortunate story is simple. Please ensure the contractor's supervisory staff has conducted a full test prior to advising you of "completion". This will save you time, energy and depending upon the season, a whole lot of sweat.

4. Employee Training: Upon the successful inspection and testing of the system we are now ready to train onsite personnel. The training should be conducted within the systems command center or onsite monitoring station. Training parameters should include an overview of the system's capabilities and each individual person should be afforded operational hands-on experience with each component. Depending upon the complexities of the system and the number of trainees, programs may last only two hours or spaced over multi-tiered, multi-day seminars.

5. Project Signoff: Once we have a fully functioning system and all employees have been adequately trained, we are now ready to finalize the project. This "turnover" from contractor to client has its own process. Outlined below are key elements for a successful completion strategy.

A. Component Documentation: Each component within the system will have its own manufacturer user's manual and other documentation. These items should be kept with the original project file.

B. Software Records & Media: Elements surrounding installed software, including manuals, license agreements and hardcopy media (such as original DVD's and CD's) should be kept and stored. Additional copies of manufacturer specific software for recording devices should be requested and are usually available free of charge.

C. Client's Property: Identification badges, keyfobs and/or issued keys should be collected from the contractor upon the completion of the project.

D. Final Signoff Documentation and Invoice: The final paperwork for completing a project can be as simple as a "Customer Satisfaction Survey" presented by the contractor or a formalized document created by your counsel. I highly discourage the signing of a formalized letter, generated by the contractor, containing contractual language within the document. Prior to signing such document, it is imperative to present it to your corporate counsel. Language contained within may negate and/or change aspects of the prearranged service agreement or maintenance schedule.

A Final Note:

Wow! Throughout our process, we have now systematically identified our threats facing us today, determined our legal and moral obligations, conducted our vulnerability assessment, established a realistic budget, wrote and presented a dynamite specification and accomplished a thorough RFP process. In addition, we have negotiated a fair and balanced contract, managed a successful installation and avoided all of the pitfalls shown within the examples.

We are good, but are we finished?

Well...yes and no.

The world around us is ever-changing and at times very fluid. Today's threats are forever evolving and changing throughout our daily life.

New emerging threats are rapidly becoming the "new norm" and we must develop countermeasures to defend ourselves and protect the ones we have both a legal and moral obligation to protect. We must constantly and consistently reexamine our protection methodologies and adjust them accordingly. A key piece of the process involves periodically updating our vulnerability assessment. This will ensure we continue to counter new and evolving threats. Another component involves upgrading and, at a minimum, maintaining our installed protection systems.

So....yes, we are finished with this particular project and no, our work to protect "our people" continues...

APPENDIX

A	**SAMPLE RESIDENTIAL PROTECTION PROPOSAL**
B	**SAMPLE SPECIFICATION ADJUSTMENT REQUEST**
C	**SAMPLE BEST AND FINAL OFFER DOCUMENT**

CRIMINAL INTELLIGENCE ADMINISTRATION
38-11 Ditmars Boulevard ▪ Astoria, New York 11105
Telephone: 718.541.0723 ▪ Toll Free: 800.792.7181 ▪ Facsimile: 718.504.7530
Email: ceo@protect.nyc   www.protect.nyc

RESIDENTIAL PROTECTION PROPOSAL

Solicitation Identification:	RFP-00000000-R/O
Site Identification:	XYZ Corporation
Physical Location:	XXXX East Anywhere Avenue
	Any Town, State 12345
Solicitation Issued:	February 2, 20xx @ 9:00 AM
Proposal Deadline:	March 15, 20xx @ 5:00 PM

LEGAL BUSINESS NAME   D/B/A

CORPORATE ADDRESS   CITY   STATE   ZIP

TELEPHONE   FACSIMILE   WEBSITE

CONTACT PERSON   TITLE   TELEPHONE   EMAIL ADDRESS

CORPORATE PRESIDENT   TELEPHONE   EMAIL ADDRESS

DUNS NUMBER(S)   CAGE CODE   EIN   NYS DOS LICENSE NUMBER   EXPIRATION

STATE OF INCORPORATION   YEAR   PRIOR CORPORATE NAME (IF CHANGED WITHIN THE PRECEDING SEVEN YEARS)

PARENT COMPANY (IF ANY)   CORPORATE ADDRESS   CITY   STATE   ZIP

TELEPHONE   FACSIMILE   WEBSITE

HAS THE CORPORATION FILED FOR BANKRUPTCY PROTECTION WITHIN THE LAST 5 YEARS?   Y ☐   N ☐

HAS THE CORPORATION EVER BEEN FOUND GUILTY OF A CRIMINAL ACT?   Y ☐   N ☐

DOES THE CORPORATION CONDUCT PRE-EMPLOYMENT BACKGROUND INVESTIGATIONS?   Y ☐   N ☐
☐ 7 YEAR CRIMINAL HISTORY   ☐ RESIDENCE VERIFICATION   ☐ CREDIT CHECK
☐ DMV LICENSE CHECK   ☐ SSN VERIFICATION   ☐ REFERENCE CHECK

OTHER(S) _____

DOES THE COMPANY HAVE A DRUG AND ALCOHOL POLICY IN EFFECT?   Y ☐ N ☐

ARE COMPANY EMPLOYEES BONDED? Y ☐ N ☐ WILL BONDED EMPLOYEES WORK ON THIS PROJECT? Y ☐ N ☐

BONDING COMPANY	ADDRESS	CITY	STATE	ZIP
TELEPHONE	FACSIMILE	WEBSITE		
CONTACT PERSON	TITLE	TELEPHONE	EMAIL ADDRESS	

DOES THE CORPORATION HAVE THE ABILITY TO ACQUIRE A PERFORMANCE BOND FOR THIS PROJECT?   Y ☐ N ☐

IF SO, WHAT IS THE CURRENT BONDING LEVEL OF THE CORPORATION? $ _____

BONDING COMPANY	ADDRESS	CITY	STATE	ZIP
TELEPHONE	FACSIMILE	WEBSITE		
CONTACT PERSON	TITLE	TELEPHONE	EMAIL ADDRESS	

CORPORATE ENTITIES PERFORMING WORK WITHIN XYZ CORPORATION WILL NEED TO MAINTAIN, IN FULL FORCE AND EFFECT, ACTIVE INSURANCE POLICIES FOR THE DURATION OF THE PROJECT AND ANY EXTENSIONS AS PER SERVICE AGREEMENTS. THE POLICIES WILL NEED TO INCLUDE COMPREHENSIVE GENERAL LIABILITY AND AUTOMOBILE LIABILITY INSURANCE IN THE AMOUNT OF NOT LESS THAN $1,000,000.(ONE MILLION USD)PER OCCURRENCE. IN ADDITION, CONTRACTORS WILL ALSO BE REQUIRED TO MAINTAIN ACTIVE WORKERS COMPENSATION AND DISABILITY INSURANCE POLICIES FOR THEIR EMPLOYEES PERFORMING WORK WITHIN THE BUILDINGS. ALL POLICIES SHOULD NOT BE SUBJECT TO CANCELLATION, NON-RENEWAL, REDUCTION IN POLICY TERMS OR OTHERWISE CHANGE IN COVERAGE FOR THE DURATION OF THE CONTRACT. APPLICABLE POLICIES WILL NEED TO INCLUDE XYZ CORPORATION AND OTHERS, AS MAY BE REQUIRED, AS ADDITIONAL INSURED.

DOES YOUR ORGANIZATION HAVE INSURANCE POLICIES IN EFFECT AS PER THE ABOVE GUIDELINES?   Y ☐ N ☐

INSURANCE COMPANY	ADDRESS	CITY	STATE	ZIP
TELEPHONE	FACSIMILE	WEBSITE		
CONTACT PERSON	TITLE	TELEPHONE	EMAIL ADDRESS	

** ATTACHMENT REQUIRED – CERTIFICATE OF INSURANCE **

DOES THE CORPORATION INTEND TO ENTER INTO SUBCONTRACTING AGREEMENTS WITH OTHER INDIVIDUALS OR BUSINESS ENTITIES FOR THE PURPOSE OF COMPLETING THE PROJECT?   Y ☐   N ☐

IF YES, SUBCONTRACTORS WILL BE BOUND BY REQUIREMENTS AND PARAMETERS CONTAINED WITHIN THIS DOCUMENT.

SUBCONTRACTOR 1: PORTION OF PROJECT_____

LEGAL BUSINESS NAME		D/B/A	
CORPORATE ADDRESS	CITY	STATE	ZIP
TELEPHONE	FACSIMILE	WEBSITE	
CONTACT PERSON	TITLE	TELEPHONE	EMAIL ADDRESS
DUNS NUMBER(S)	CAGE CODE	EIN	NYS DOS LICENSE NUMBER EXPIRATION
STATE OF INCORPORATION	YEAR	PRIOR CORPORATE NAME (IF CHANGED WITHIN THE PRECEDING SEVEN YEARS)	
PARENT COMPANY (IF ANY)	CORPORATE ADDRESS	CITY STATE	ZIP
TELEPHONE	FACSIMILE	WEBSITE	

HAS THE CORPORATION FILED FOR BANKRUPTCY PROTECTION WITHIN THE LAST 5 YEARS?   Y ☐   N ☐

HAS THE CORPORATION EVER BEEN FOUND GUILTY OF A CRIMINAL ACT?   Y ☐   N ☐

DOES THE CORPORATION CONDUCT PRE-EMPLOYMENT BACKGROUND INVESTIGATIONS?   Y ☐   N ☐
☐ 7 YEAR CRIMINAL HISTORY   ☐ RESIDENCE VERIFICATION   ☐ CREDIT CHECK
☐ DMV LICENSE CHECK   ☐ SSN VERIFICATION   ☐ REFERENCE CHECK

OTHER(S) _____

DOES THE COMPANY HAVE A DRUG AND ALCOHOL POLICY IN EFFECT?   Y ☐ N ☐

ARE COMPANY EMPLOYEES BONDED? Y ☐   N ☐   WILL BONDED EMPLOYEES WORK ON THIS PROJECT? Y ☐ N ☐

DOES THIS ORGANIZATION HAVE INSURANCE POLICIES IN EFFECT AS PER THE GUIDELINES?   Y ☐ N ☐

INSURANCE COMPANY	ADDRESS	CITY	STATE	ZIP

TELEPHONE	FACSIMILE	WEBSITE	

CONTACT PERSON	TITLE	TELEPHONE	EMAIL ADDRESS

SUBCONTRACTOR 2: PORTION OF PROJECT

LEGAL BUSINESS NAME		D/B/A	

CORPORATE ADDRESS	CITY	STATE	ZIP

TELEPHONE	FACSIMILE	WEBSITE	

CONTACT PERSON	TITLE	TELEPHONE	EMAIL ADDRESS

DUNS NUMBER(S)	CAGE CODE	EIN	NYS DOS LICENSE NUMBER	EXPIRATION

STATE OF INCORPORATION	YEAR	PRIOR CORPORATE NAME (IF CHANGED WITHIN THE PRECEDING SEVEN YEARS)

PARENT COMPANY (IF ANY)	CORPORATE ADDRESS	CITY	STATE	ZIP

TELEPHONE	FACSIMILE	WEBSITE	

HAS THE CORPORATION FILED FOR BANKRUPTCY PROTECTION WITHIN THE LAST 5 YEARS?　Y ☐　N ☐

HAS THE CORPORATION EVER BEEN FOUND GUILTY OF A CRIMINAL ACT?　Y ☐　N ☐

DOES THE CORPORATION CONDUCT PRE-EMPLOYMENT BACKGROUND INVESTIGATIONS?　Y ☐　N ☐
☐ 7 YEAR CRIMINAL HISTORY　☐ RESIDENCE VERIFICATION　☐ CREDIT CHECK
☐ DMV LICENSE CHECK　☐ SSN VERIFICATION　☐ REFERENCE CHECK

OTHER(S) _____

DOES THE COMPANY HAVE A DRUG AND ALCOHOL POLICY IN EFFECT?　Y ☐ N ☐

ARE COMPANY EMPLOYEES BONDED? Y ☐　N ☐　WILL BONDED EMPLOYEES WORK ON THIS PROJECT? Y ☐ N ☐

DOES THIS ORGANIZATION HAVE INSURANCE POLICIES IN EFFECT AS PER THE GUIDELINES?　Y ☐ N ☐

INSURANCE COMPANY	ADDRESS	CITY	STATE	ZIP

TELEPHONE	FACSIMILE	WEBSITE	

CONTACT PERSON	TITLE	TELEPHONE	EMAIL ADDRESS

SUBCONTRACTOR 3: PORTION OF PROJECT_____

LEGAL BUSINESS NAME		D/B/A	

CORPORATE ADDRESS	CITY	STATE	ZIP

TELEPHONE	FACSIMILE	WEBSITE

CONTACT PERSON	TITLE	TELEPHONE	EMAIL ADDRESS

DUNS NUMBER(S)	CAGE CODE	EIN	NYS DOS LICENSE NUMBER	EXPIRATION

STATE OF INCORPORATION	YEAR	PRIOR CORPORATE NAME (IF CHANGED WITHIN THE PRECEDING SEVEN YEARS)

PARENT COMPANY (IF ANY)	CORPORATE ADDRESS	CITY	STATE	ZIP

TELEPHONE	FACSIMILE	WEBSITE

HAS THE CORPORATION FILED FOR BANKRUPTCY PROTECTION WITHIN THE LAST 5 YEARS?   Y ☐   N ☐

HAS THE CORPORATION EVER BEEN FOUND GUILTY OF A CRIMINAL ACT?   Y ☐   N ☐

DOES THE CORPORATION CONDUCT PRE-EMPLOYMENT BACKGROUND INVESTIGATIONS?   Y ☐   N ☐
☐ 7 YEAR CRIMINAL HISTORY   ☐ RESIDENCE VERIFICATION   ☐ CREDIT CHECK
☐ DMV LICENSE CHECK   ☐ SSN VERIFICATION   ☐ REFERENCE CHECK

OTHER(S)_____

DOES THE COMPANY HAVE A DRUG AND ALCOHOL POLICY IN EFFECT?   Y ☐ N ☐

ARE COMPANY EMPLOYEES BONDED? Y ☐   N ☐   WILL BONDED EMPLOYEES WORK ON THIS PROJECT? Y ☐ N ☐

DOES THIS ORGANIZATION HAVE INSURANCE POLICIES IN EFFECT AS PER THE GUIDELINES?   Y ☐ N ☐

INSURANCE COMPANY	ADDRESS	CITY	STATE	ZIP

TELEPHONE	FACSIMILE	WEBSITE

CONTACT PERSON	TITLE	TELEPHONE	EMAIL ADDRESS

SUBCONTRACTOR 4: PORTION OF PROJECT_____

LEGAL BUSINESS NAME	D/B/A

CORPORATE ADDRESS	CITY	STATE	ZIP

TELEPHONE	FACSIMILE	WEBSITE

CONTACT PERSON	TITLE	TELEPHONE	EMAIL ADDRESS

DUNS NUMBER(S)	CAGE CODE	EIN	NYS DOS LICENSE NUMBER	EXPIRATION

STATE OF INCORPORATION	YEAR	PRIOR CORPORATE NAME (IF CHANGED WITHIN THE PRECEDING SEVEN YEARS)

PARENT COMPANY (IF ANY)	CORPORATE ADDRESS	CITY	STATE	ZIP

TELEPHONE	FACSIMILE	WEBSITE

HAS THE CORPORATION FILED FOR BANKRUPTCY PROTECTION WITHIN THE LAST 5 YEARS?   Y ☐   N ☐

HAS THE CORPORATION EVER BEEN FOUND GUILTY OF A CRIMINAL ACT?   Y ☐   N ☐

DOES THE CORPORATION CONDUCT PRE-EMPLOYMENT BACKGROUND INVESTIGATIONS?   Y ☐   N ☐
☐ 7 YEAR CRIMINAL HISTORY   ☐ RESIDENCE VERIFICATION   ☐ CREDIT CHECK
☐ DMV LICENSE CHECK   ☐ SSN VERIFICATION   ☐ REFERENCE CHECK

OTHER(S) _____

DOES THE COMPANY HAVE A DRUG AND ALCOHOL POLICY IN EFFECT?   Y ☐ N ☐

ARE COMPANY EMPLOYEES BONDED? Y ☐   N ☐   WILL BONDED EMPLOYEES WORK ON THIS PROJECT? Y ☐ N ☐

DOES THIS ORGANIZATION HAVE INSURANCE POLICIES IN EFFECT AS PER THE GUIDELINES?   Y ☐ N ☐

INSURANCE COMPANY	ADDRESS	CITY	STATE	ZIP

TELEPHONE	FACSIMILE	WEBSITE

CONTACT PERSON	TITLE	TELEPHONE	EMAIL ADDRESS

SUBCONTRACTOR 5: PORTION OF PROJECT_____

LEGAL BUSINESS NAME			D/B/A	

CORPORATE ADDRESS	CITY	STATE		ZIP

TELEPHONE	FACSIMILE	WEBSITE	

CONTACT PERSON	TITLE	TELEPHONE	EMAIL ADDRESS

DUNS NUMBER(S)	CAGE CODE	EIN	NYS DOS LICENSE NUMBER	EXPIRATION

STATE OF INCORPORATION	YEAR	PRIOR CORPORATE NAME (IF CHANGED WITHIN THE PRECEDING SEVEN YEARS)

PARENT COMPANY (IF ANY)	CORPORATE ADDRESS	CITY	STATE	ZIP

TELEPHONE	FACSIMILE	WEBSITE

HAS THE CORPORATION FILED FOR BANKRUPTCY PROTECTION WITHIN THE LAST 5 YEARS?   Y ☐   N ☐

HAS THE CORPORATION EVER BEEN FOUND GUILTY OF A CRIMINAL ACT?   Y ☐   N ☐

DOES THE CORPORATION CONDUCT PRE-EMPLOYMENT BACKGROUND INVESTIGATIONS?   Y ☐   N ☐
☐ 7 YEAR CRIMINAL HISTORY   ☐ RESIDENCE VERIFICATION   ☐ CREDIT CHECK
☐ DMV LICENSE CHECK   ☐ SSN VERIFICATION   ☐ REFERENCE CHECK

OTHER(S)_____

DOES THE COMPANY HAVE A DRUG AND ALCOHOL POLICY IN EFFECT?   Y ☐ N ☐

ARE COMPANY EMPLOYEES BONDED? Y ☐   N ☐   WILL BONDED EMPLOYEES WORK ON THIS PROJECT? Y ☐ N ☐

DOES THIS ORGANIZATION HAVE INSURANCE POLICIES IN EFFECT AS PER THE GUIDELINES?   Y ☐ N ☐

INSURANCE COMPANY	ADDRESS	CITY	STATE	ZIP

TELEPHONE	FACSIMILE	WEBSITE

CONTACT PERSON	TITLE	TELEPHONE	EMAIL ADDRESS

THIS PROJECT WILL REQUIRE MULTIPLE WORK CREWS CONCURRENTLY WORKING ON ALL PORTIONS OF THIS PROJECT. HOW MANY WORK CREWS WILL BE ASSIGNED TO THE FOLLOWING PORTION?

DIGITAL IMAGING SYSTEM: _____ WORK CREWS _____ TOTAL PERSONS/CREW _____ SUPERVISORS

THIS PROJECT DOES NOT SPECIFY MANDATORY UNION LABOR. IN ORDER TO ASSESS THE COST PARAMETERS OF YOUR PROPOSAL, PLEASE INDICATE ONE OF THE FOLLOWING:

☐   OUR ORGANIZATION WILL ONLY UTILIZE UNION LABOR FOR THIS PROJECT

☐   OUR ORGANIZATION WILL UTILIZE NON-UNION LABOR

THIS PROJECT WILL ALSO REQUIRE AN ON-SITE INSTALLATION MANAGER TO ENSURE A SEAMLESS INSTALLATION.

NAME OF PROPOSED INSTALLATION MANAGER (IF AVAILABLE DURING RFP)_____

IN ORDER TO ENSURE PROPERLY INSTALLED AND SERVICED SYSTEMS, THIS PROJECT WILL REQUIRE ENTITIES RESPONDING TO THIS RFP TO BE AUTHORIZED MANUFACTURES REPRESENTATIVES FOR ALL PROPOSED SYSTEM COMPONENTS.

ARE YOU AN AUTHORIZED MANUFACTURES REPRESENTATIVE FOR YOUR PROPOSED SYSTEM COMPONENTS? ☐ Y ☐ N

IF APPLICABLE, DID YOUR ORGANIZATION COMPLETE MANDATED TRAINING PROGRAMS AS PER MANUFACTURER REQUIREMENTS? ☐ Y ☐ N

PLEASE INDICATE THE ESTIMATED LEAD/COMPLETION TIMEFRAMES REQUIRED FOR THE APPLICABLE SYSTEM:

DIGITAL IMAGING SYSTEM: LEAD TIME FRAME ___ DAYS - COMPLETION TIME FRAME ___ MONTHS

ESTIMATED TIMEFRAME FOR TOTAL PROJECT COMPLETION_____

COMMENTS: _____

_____

_____

_____

_____

_____

_____

_____

SCHEDULES OF COSTS, FEES AND SERVICES:

THE FOLLOWING SCHEDULES WILL BE BINDING AND REFLECT A TRUE AND ACCURATE ACCOUNT OF ALL COSTS, FEES AND SERVICES REQUIRED FOR COMPLETE INSTALLATION OF FULLY OPERATIONAL SPECIFIED SYSTEMS. THE FOLLOWING WILL NEED TO BE CONSISTENT WITH ANY AND ALL PROPRIETARY/ORGANIZATION-SPECIFIC PROPOSALS SUBMITTED.

DIGITAL IMAGING SYSTEM

A. INTERIOR SURVEILLANCE CAMERAS - FIXED

MANUFACTURER	MODEL NUMBER	DESCRIPTION	UNINSTALLED UNIT COST

B. ELEVATOR SURVEILLANCE CAMERAS - FIXED

MANUFACTURER	MODEL NUMBER	DESCRIPTION	UNINSTALLED UNIT COST

C. INTERIOR SURVEILLANCE CAMERAS - PTZ

MANUFACTURER	MODEL NUMBER	DESCRIPTION	UNINSTALLED UNIT COST

D. EXTERIOR SURVEILLANCE CAMERAS

MANUFACTURER	MODEL NUMBER	DESCRIPTION	UNINSTALLED UNIT COST

E. TRANSCEIVERS/POWER SUPPLIES

MANUFACTURER	MODEL NUMBER	DESCRIPTION	UNINSTALLED UNIT COST

F. DIGITAL VIDEO RECORDERS

MANUFACTURER	MODEL NUMBER	DESCRIPTION	UNINSTALLED UNIT COST

G. MONITORING EQUIPMENT

MANUFACTURER	MODEL NUMBER	DESCRIPTION	UNINSTALLED UNIT COST

H. MONITORING PANEL

MANUFACTURER	MODEL NUMBER	DESCRIPTION	UNINSTALLED UNIT COST

I. INSTALLATION COSTS

ITEM DESCRIPTION	TOTAL INSTALLED COST
SURVEILLANCE SYSTEM COMPONENTS	$
MONITORING PANEL	$
ELECTRICAL CONNECTIVITY/SURGE PROTECTION	$
PLASTER, PATCH AND REPAIR	$
DEBRIS REMOVAL	$
EMPLOYEE TRAINING	$
MISCELLANEOUS COSTS AND FEES	$
TOTAL INSTALLED SURVEILLANCE SYSTEM	$

J. MISCELLANEOUS FEES AND EXPENSES - POST-INSTALLATION

ITEM DESCRIPTION	TOTAL COST/COST PER HOUR
TECHNICAL ASSISTANCE/INSTALLED SOFTWARE	$
GENERAL HOURLY BILL RATE FOR SERVICES	$
	$
	$
	$

K. MISCELLANEOUS ITEMS

DO INSTALLED COMPONENTS OFFER A MANUFACTURERS WARRANTEE? ☐ Y ☐ N

PLEASE INDICATE APPLICABLE WARRANTEE INFORMATION

SURVEILLANCE CAMERAS _____ YEAR(S) SYSTEM CABLES/WIRING/POWER _____ YEAR(S)

DIGITAL VIDEO RECORDERS _____ YEAR(S) MONITORING EQUIPMENT _____ YEAR(S)

MONITORING PANEL _____ YEAR(S) ELECTRICAL CONNECTIVITY/SURGE PROTECTION _____ YEAR(S)

DOES YOUR ORGANIZATION OFFER AN ANNUAL SERVICE/MAINTENANCE PLAN? ☐ Y ☐ N

WHAT IS THE COST FOR AN ANNUAL AGREEMENT? $_____ P/YEAR

IS THERE A CANCELLATION CLAUSE? ☐ Y ☐ N

WHAT TIMEFRAME IS ALLOTTED FOR CANCELLATION ONCE THE AGREEMENT IS INITIATED? _____

IF SYSTEM COMPONENTS FAIL AND NEED TO BE REMOVED FROM THE SITE, DO YOU HAVE LOANER EQUIPMENT AVAILABLE UNTIL THE SYSTEM IS REPAIRED? ☐ Y ☐ N

ARE THERE ASSOCIATED COSTS WITH THE LOANER EQUIPMENT? ☐ Y ☐ N

COMMENTS: _____

CLIENT REFERENCES:

REFERENCE 1.

TYPE OF INSTALLATION/SERVICE			TOTAL DOLLAR AMOUNT	
BUSINESS NAME	ADDRESS	CITY	STATE	ZIP
TELEPHONE	FACSIMILE		WEBSITE	
CONTACT PERSON	TITLE	TELEPHONE	EMAIL ADDRESS	

REFERENCE 2.

TYPE OF INSTALLATION/SERVICE			TOTAL DOLLAR AMOUNT	
BUSINESS NAME	ADDRESS	CITY	STATE	ZIP
TELEPHONE	FACSIMILE		WEBSITE	
CONTACT PERSON	TITLE	TELEPHONE	EMAIL ADDRESS	

REFERENCE 3.

TYPE OF INSTALLATION/SERVICE			TOTAL DOLLAR AMOUNT	
BUSINESS NAME	ADDRESS	CITY	STATE	ZIP

TELEPHONE	FACSIMILE		WEBSITE	

CONTACT PERSON	TITLE	TELEPHONE	EMAIL ADDRESS

REFERENCE 4.

TYPE OF INSTALLATION/SERVICE		TOTAL DOLLAR AMOUNT

BUSINESS NAME	ADDRESS	CITY	STATE	ZIP

TELEPHONE	FACSIMILE		WEBSITE	

CONTACT PERSON	TITLE	TELEPHONE	EMAIL ADDRESS

REFERENCE 5.

TYPE OF INSTALLATION/SERVICE		TOTAL DOLLAR AMOUNT

BUSINESS NAME	ADDRESS	CITY	STATE	ZIP

TELEPHONE	FACSIMILE		WEBSITE	

CONTACT PERSON	TITLE	TELEPHONE	EMAIL ADDRESS

REFERENCE 6.

TYPE OF INSTALLATION/SERVICE		TOTAL DOLLAR AMOUNT

BUSINESS NAME	ADDRESS	CITY	STATE	ZIP

TELEPHONE	FACSIMILE		WEBSITE	

CONTACT PERSON	TITLE	TELEPHONE	EMAIL ADDRESS

REFERENCE 7.

TYPE OF INSTALLATION/SERVICE				TOTAL DOLLAR AMOUNT	
BUSINESS NAME		ADDRESS	CITY	STATE	ZIP
TELEPHONE	FACSIMILE		WEBSITE		
CONTACT PERSON	TITLE		TELEPHONE	EMAIL ADDRESS	

REFERENCE 8.

TYPE OF INSTALLATION/SERVICE				TOTAL DOLLAR AMOUNT	
BUSINESS NAME		ADDRESS	CITY	STATE	ZIP
TELEPHONE	FACSIMILE		WEBSITE		
CONTACT PERSON	TITLE		TELEPHONE	EMAIL ADDRESS	

REFERENCE 9.

TYPE OF INSTALLATION/SERVICE				TOTAL DOLLAR AMOUNT	
BUSINESS NAME		ADDRESS	CITY	STATE	ZIP
TELEPHONE	FACSIMILE		WEBSITE		
CONTACT PERSON	TITLE		TELEPHONE	EMAIL ADDRESS	

REFERENCE 10.

TYPE OF INSTALLATION/SERVICE				TOTAL DOLLAR AMOUNT	
BUSINESS NAME		ADDRESS	CITY	STATE	ZIP

TELEPHONE	FACSIMILE		WEBSITE

CONTACT PERSON	TITLE	TELEPHONE	EMAIL ADDRESS

REFERENCE 11.

TYPE OF INSTALLATION/SERVICE	TOTAL DOLLAR AMOUNT

BUSINESS NAME	ADDRESS	CITY	STATE	ZIP

TELEPHONE	FACSIMILE	WEBSITE

CONTACT PERSON	TITLE	TELEPHONE	EMAIL ADDRESS

TOTAL PROPOSED COST

ITEM DESCRIPTION	TOTAL ASSOCIATED COST
DIGITAL IMAGING SYSTEM	$

TOTAL COST FOR PROTECTION UPGRADE (DO NOT INCLUDE TAX) $_____

PAYMENT TERMS

PAYMENT TYPE	TIME FRAME	PAYMENT DUE	COMMENTS
		$	
		$	
		$	
		$	

REQUIRED ATTACHMENTS

THE FOLLOWING DOCUMENTATION WILL NEED TO BE SUBMITTED:

1. COMPLETED AND SIGNED RESIDENTIAL PROTECTION PROPOSAL
2. COPY OF CURRENT INSURANCE CERTIFICATES
3. MANUFACTURES SPECIFICATION SHEETS AND BROCHURES FOR PROPOSED SYSTEM COMPONENTS
4. PROPRIETARY/ORGANIZATION-SPECIFIC PROPOSALS
5. SPECIFICATION ADJUSTMENT REQUEST FORM

I CERTIFY THAT I HAVE READ AND FULLY UNDERSTAND THE ENCLOSED SPECIFICATION DOCUMENT FOR THE OUTLINED INSTALLATION SERVICES. I FURTHER CERTIFY THAT I HAVE SUBMITTED THE PROPER DOCUMENTATION AS REQUESTED AND I AM AUTHORIZED TO ENTER INTO AN AGREEMENT AND BINDING CONTRACT FOR THE ORGANIZATION DEFINED WITHIN THIS

DOCUMENT. I UNDERSTAND THAT THIS DOCUMENT REPRESENTS ONLY A PROPOSAL AND NOT AN AUTHORIZATION TO COMMENCE WORK.

I FURTHER UNDERSTAND AND IT IS AGREED THAT XYZ CORPORATION MAY ELECT TO MODIFY THE SPECIFICATION AT ANY TIME AND/OR TERMINATE THE PROJECT ALTOGETHER. IT IS UNDERSTOOD AND AGREED THAT XYZ CORPORATION IS UNDER NO OBLIGATION TO PURSUE INSTALLATION SERVICES FOR THIS SOLICITATION.

IN ADDITION, IT IS UNDERSTOOD AND AGREED THE AWARDED CONTRACTOR WILL HAVE THE ULTIMATE RESPONSIBILITY TO ENSURE ALL SYSTEMS ARE COMPLETELY OPERATIONAL AND IS IN COMPLIANCE WITH ELECTRICAL AND/OR BUILDING CODE REQUIREMENTS AS WELL AS APPLICABLE LAWS.

SIGNED THIS _____ DAY OF _____ 20__   AS AGENT FOR: _____

_____   ADDRESS: _____
SIGNATURE OF AUTHORIZED REPRESENTATIVE

                                             _____

_____   TELEPHONE: _____
PRINT NAME AND CORPORATE TITLE

CRIMINAL INTELLIGENCE ADMINISTRATION

38-11 Ditmars Boulevard ▪ Astoria, New York 11105
Telephone: 718.541.0723 ▪ Toll Free: 800.792.7181 ▪ Facsimile: 718.504.7530
Email: ceo@protect.nyc   www.protect.nyc

SPECIFICATION ADJUSTMENT REQUEST

Solicitation Identification:	RFP-00000000-R/O
Site Identification:	XYZ Corporation
Physical Location:	XXXX East Anywhere Avenue
	Any Town, State 12345
Solicitation Issued:	February 2, 20xx @ 9:00 AM
Proposal Deadline:	March 15, 20xx @ 5:00 PM

REQUEST DATE: _____

BUSINESS NAME	ADDRESS	CITY	STATE	ZIP
TELEPHONE	FACSIMILE	WEBSITE		
CONTACT PERSON	TITLE	TELEPHONE	EMAIL	

THE FOLLOWING SPECIFICATION ADJUSTMENTS ARE REQUESTED:

PAGE #	ADJUSTMENT REQUEST	REASON	PROPOSED ACTION

CRIMINAL INTELLIGENCE ADMINISTRATION
38-11 Ditmars Boulevard ▪ Astoria, New York 11105
Telephone: 718.541.0723 ▪ Toll Free: 800.792.7181 ▪ Facsimile: 718.504.7530
Email: ceo@protect.nyc   www.protect.nyc

BEST AND FINAL OFFER

Solicitation Identification:	RFP-00000000-R/O
Site Identification:	XYZ Corporation
Physical Location:	XXXX East Anywhere Avenue
	Any Town, State 12345
Solicitation Issued:	February 2, 20xx @ 9:00 AM
Proposal Deadline:	March 15, 20xx @ 5:00 PM

ENTITY IDENTIFICATION: _____

_____

I CERTIFY THAT I HAVE READ AND FULLY UNDERSTAND THE SPECIFICATION DOCUMENTS FOR THE ABOVE REFERENCED SOLICITATION. I FURTHER CERTIFY THAT I HAVE SUBMITTED THE PROPER DOCUMENTATION AS REQUESTED AND I AM AUTHORIZED TO ENTER INTO AN AGREEMENT AND BINDING CONTRACT FOR THE ORGANIZATION DEFINED WITHIN THIS DOCUMENT. I UNDERSTAND THAT THIS DOCUMENT REPRESENTS ONLY A PROPOSAL AND NOT AN AUTHORIZATION TO COMMENCE WORK.

IN ADDITION, IT IS UNDERSTOOD AND AGREED THE AWARDED CONTRACTOR WILL HAVE THE ULTIMATE RESPONSIBILITY TO ENSURE ALL SYSTEMS ARE COMPLETELY OPERATIONAL AND IS IN COMPLIANCE WITH ELECTRICAL AND/OR BUILDING CODE REQUIREMENTS AS WELL AS APPLICABLE LAWS.

_____

DIGITAL IMAGING SYSTEM:

    A. TOTAL INSTALLED COST: $ _____

    B. PERFORMANCE & PAYMENT BOND COSTS: $ _____

    ---------------TOTAL COST: $ _____

    C. ANNUAL MAINTENANCE/SERVICE AGREEMENT COST: $ _____

_____

I FURTHER CERTIFY THE ABOVE PRICING SCHEDULE REFLECTS A TRUE AND ACCURATE ACCOUNT FOR THE COMPLETE INSTALLATION OF THE ENTIRE DIGITAL IMAGING SYSTEM. IN ADDITION, IT IS AGREED THE NOTED SERVICE AGREEMENT WILL BE IMPLEMENTED AND CHARGED UPON THE SECOND YEAR FOLLOWING INSTALLATION. THE FIRST TWELVE (12) MONTHS AFTER INSTALLATION WILL NOT INCUR ANY CHARGE FOR REPLACEMENT AND/OR REPAIR OF DEFECTIVE/FAILED SYSTEM COMPONENTS.

SIGNED THIS _____ DAY OF _____ 20__   AS AGENT FOR:_____

_____   ADDRESS:_____

SIGNATURE OF AUTHORIZED REPRESENTATIVE

                                                       _____

_____

PRINT NAME AND CORPORATE TITLE   TELEPHONE:_____